The Chimes of Shreveport

Jewel Mae Daniel

Numbers 6:24-26

The Chimes of Shreveport

THE LIFE OF

M. E. Dodd

THE HEART OF THE COOPERATIVE PROGRAM

Jewel Mae Daniel

PROVIDENCE HOUSE PUBLISHERS
Franklin, Tennessee

Printed in the United States of America

05   04   03   02   01   1   2   3   4   5

Library of Congress Catalog Card Number: 2001091671

ISBN: 1-57736-244-6

Cover design by Gary Bozeman

The tower depicted on the cover is the ten-story structure that housed the original "chimes of Shreveport"—thirteen bells that rang out from the First Baptist Church at Travis and McNeil streets in downtown Shreveport, Louisiana.

All scripture quotations are taken from the HOLY BIBLE, King James Version.

PROVIDENCE HOUSE PUBLISHERS
238 Seaboard Lane • Franklin, Tennessee 37067
800-321-5692
www.providencehouse.com

In memory of
Larry Daniel, my husband;
Jewel Storms Rice Carruth, my mother;
Gordon L. Rice, my father;
and Dr. Richard Ellsworth Day, my mentor.
and
To
My children Gary and Darlene Maroney,
Deborah Day Daniel,
and Gordon and Joan Daniel.

Contents

Foreword

M. E. DODD. THE NAME DID NOT REGISTER WITH ME UNTIL I became a student at New Orleans Baptist Theological Seminary. I noted that one of the student residences was named M. E. Dodd Hall. My ignorance continued for a while, but I began to hear the name referenced in classes and in my reading of Baptist history. After seminary graduation, I had the opportunity to preach at the First Baptist Church of Shreveport, Louisiana, where I was reminded that this man had pastored the church for thirty-eight years. That will get any pastor's attention!

As my involvement with Southern Baptist life grew, my sensitivity to the powerful ministry of the Cooperative Program was sharpened. The churches I pastored had dutifully sent money to Baptist work through the Cooperative Program, but I had taken that for granted. I knew of several of its strengths, including helping underwrite a quality education program in one of our seminaries. I also knew it was the lifeline in the lengthening shadow of our mission involvement. The more I knew about it, the more convinced I was that the church I pastored should heartily support and endorse it. The more I knew of the support system other denominations used to accomplish their mission, the more I realized that we as Southern Baptists had a unique system that could only have its genesis in a God-engendered vision. That vision was the heartbeat of M. E. Dodd, the founder of my alma mater, New Orleans Baptist Theological Seminary, and the driving force for the launching of the Cooperative Program.

I was overwhelmed when I was chosen to be the first recipient of the Executive Committee's M. E. Dodd Award, given to me at the Southern Baptist Convention in Orlando, Florida, in June 2000. The things we felt the Lord Jesus had led us to do seemed but a match beside the torch he lit and carried. Here was a man who was the epitome of a pastor and preacher, who touched the world through his mission efforts, raised millions of dollars for the cause of Christ, and gave himself, untiringly, to God's agenda. What a mighty man of God! One of the glories of heaven will be to meet those who have preceded us in faith and death. It will be a privilege to know M. E. Dodd, whom I feel I already know because of common bonds in our Master and ministry. He was a man who left the woodpile larger than he found it. I'm sure this book will enlarge our appreciation of this pastor, who like King David, not only "served his generation well," but whose contributions continue to ripple on the lake of life.

Dr. Jim Henry
Pastor
First Baptist Church — Orlando

Dr. Henry receiving the M. E. Dodd award from Dr. Chapman, executive president of the Southern Baptist Convention in June of 2000.

Prelude

THE SOUND OF THE FOGHORNS BLOWING THEIR WARNING to the ships pierced my ears and was like a loud drum beating against my heart. It evoked thoughts that ran as deep as the San Francisco Bay, beside the Golden Gate.

We lived in the Presidio in San Francisco, and I was looking out my bedroom window. The fog was rolling in, and it could be very treacherous, for it was enfolding everything in its path—the darkness was intense. When I was growing up there beside the Golden Gate, I had no idea that my childhood would be the beginning of my writing the life story of M. E. Dodd.

Dr. Richard Ellsworth Day, the minister at Hamilton Square Baptist Church in San Francisco, was my pastor. I served as his flower girl on Sunday mornings when we offered the right hand of Christian fellowship and stood by his side as people shook his hand leaving the church. It was at this time that Dr. Day began writing two biographies: *The Shadow of the Broad Brim*, a biography of Spurgeon, and *Bush Aglow*, about Moody.

Years later, my husband and I were serving at First Baptist Church, Shreveport, Louisiana. I was Dr. Dodd's youth and drama director, and my husband served as the minister of music and education and as administrator. After fourteen years, my husband was called to be ordained and served as pastor of Horseshoe Drive Baptist Church in Alexandria, Louisiana.

Soon after we came to Shreveport, the church was holding a Bible conference, and Dr. R. E. Day was invited to speak. No one knew of my association with him as a child, and he did not know that I was in this church. Needless to say, excitement abounded in my heart as I anticipated the week of special services.

In conversation one evening, Dr. Day said to me, "Jewel Mae, Dr. Dodd should have a book written about him. I would do it, but I am already booked for several more biographies—you can do it!"

"I can't do that," I said.

The next night at church, he handed me a small folded paper, which I still have. It was a crude sample of his ideas for the book's cover, complete with title and pictures scribbled in his writing.

When Dr. Dodd celebrated his thirty-eighth anniversary as pastor of the church and his fiftieth anniversary as a minister of the gospel, I was asked to write, direct, and narrate a pageant to celebrate the monumental event. So I was not a stranger to the thought—but a biography? As I went home that evening, I felt a weight I had never felt before. Around two o'clock the next morning, I was awakened by bells ringing.

I shook my husband awake and asked, "Did you hear those bells?"

"No," he said, "I didn't hear any bells. Go back to sleep."

But I had heard them and knew Where and Whom they were from.

That was the beginning—the Lord laid it on my heart. Dr. Day was my mentor; Dr. Dodd gave me his blessing, and I worked with him until the Lord called him home. I did not know the road would be so long and sinuous, or that the foghorns I heard blowing from San Francisco Bay as a child would be bells ringing in time.

The Chimes of Shreveport features an analogy of Dr. M. E. Dodd and the thirteen bell chimes in the ten-story tower of the First Baptist Church at the downtown site in Shreveport, Louisiana. (The chimes were later moved to the church's new site at Ockley Drive.) Using the city of Shreveport is not meant to contain Dr. Dodd within a certain boundary. Quite the contrary, for many have declared him to be the chimes of the world. Shreveport was simply his home base—headquarters of a world ministry for thirty-eight years. The great Baptist pioneer for Christ that he was, Dr. Dodd would have been the chimes even if there had been no bell tower! From serving our convention as chairman of the committee that studied, researched, and finally proposed the financial support plan which still serves us today, to traveling around the globe visiting key mission points, Dr. Dodd's evangelistic zeal never waned as he relentlessly drew crowds to worship the King of Glory.

As you begin your journey through the pages of *The Chimes of Shreveport*, keep in mind that Christianity came into the world with the speech of angels. Ah, yes—on the wings of a song. That is the story being told and the only music being played within these pages. There is only one chord to strike and that chord is the Lord Jesus Christ.

Acknowledgments

I extend my most sincere appreciation to Virginia Dupree Joyner, Dr. Dodd's granddaughter, and Rev. Jim Lofton. I also wish to thank Dr. and Mrs. Robert R. Welch, to whom God gave the gift of vision. The members of Parkhills Baptist Church San Antonio, Texas, along with their pastor, are sending this message to glorify the Lord Jesus Christ. Each of them, in the most unique way, has dipped a pen in the ink.

CHORISTERS OF THE CHIMES

Dr. C. E. Autrey
Dr. James Alex Baggett
Dr. Carl Bates
Dr. and Mrs. Robert E. Beddoe
Raymond Boswell
Dr. Mary D. Bowman
Elaine H. Brister
Dr. J. Whitcomb Brougher Jr.
Kathryn E. Carpenter
Addie B. Beddoe Choate
Dr. David S. Dockery
Helen Dodd Dupree
Dr. Walter M. Fox
Dr. J. D. Grey
Dr. G. Earl Guinn
Dr. Charles Harvey
Dottie Primeaux Hayes

Dr. E. D. Head
Dr. T. L. Holcomb
Dr. C. Oscar Johnson
Belinda Kaye Keller
Dr. Charles Kelley
Dr. J. B. Lawrence
Dr. Roland Q. Leavell
Dr. R. G. Lee
Dr. Robert L. Lee
Dr. Duke McCall
Marjorie Jones McCullough
Cindy Meredith
Dr. Guy Douglas Newman
Dr. John Newport
Dr. Daniel and Beverly O'Reagan
Walter E. Price Jr.
Dr. J. Franklin Ray

Dr. Landrum Salley

Dr. Perry R. Sanders

Dr. Leonard Sanderson

Dr. Udell Smith

Dr. Ray Summers

Dr. Scott L. Tatum

Rev. Charlie Taylor

Dr. W. O. Vaught Jr.

Dr. Perry Webb Sr.

Rev. Grady E. Welch

Virginia Wingo

Dr. Kyle M. Yates

To all of the foregoing—presidents of colleges, seminaries, Baptist World Alliance, Southern Baptist Convention; professors, missionaries, pastors, heads of departments throughout the convention, architects, evangelists, family and scores of friends whose names are not printed, good members of the chimes cast—all have helped in the writing of the book with heartfelt enthusiasm. Gratitude is mine!

Sketch of M. E. Dodd
as *The Chimes of Shreveport*
by Jewel Mae Daniel

If I can heal the discord
in the hearts of men,
Or make the sour notes whole
and beautiful again.
And show them my Savior's
waiting heart of grace,
Which will bring harmony within
if they'll look upon His face.
Oh, grant it, Lord, if I can but
bring them to Thy waiting feet,
For cleansing of their souls
at Thy mercy seat.
And make salvation chime within
their yearning breasts,
And feel that with the help of God
I've preached my very best.
If I can do all these things,
my heart will certainly sing;
For this is the only kind of bell
I ever care to ring.

Ah! Ring out oh bells, for he was the chimes!

CHAPTER 1

"When a person wishes to transfer his citizenship from another country to the United States of America, there are two things necessary for him to do. He must renounce all allegiance to the old country and must accept the Constitution, the Flag, and the laws of the country in which he seeks citizenship.
It is the same in the matter of religious experience and spiritual life. In the Bible, this is called repentance and faith. In Mark 1:15, it is recorded that Jesus said, 'Repent and believe the Gospel.' Repentance means the renunciation of the old country and believing means acceptance of the new country."
—M. E. Dodd—

Let Freedom Ring

Onward, Christian Soldiers,
Marching as to war,
With the cross of Jesus
Going on before!

Listen! Those are the chimes in the tower—

Christ, the royal Master,
Leads against the foe;
Forward into battle,
See His banners go!

People are stopping to listen as the great bells, ten stories up in God's blue, continue to peal—

Like a mighty army
Moves the church of God:
Brothers, we are treading
Where the saints have trod;

The people are moving now as if being drawn by a magnet—

Onward, then, ye people,
Join our happy throng,
Blend with ours your voices
In the triumph song;
Glory, laud, and honor,

1

Unto Christ the King:
This through countless ages
Men and angels sing.

A man standing on the sidewalk heard the bells and asked a fellow passerby to direct him to the place from which the music rang.

"That is First Baptist Church. Go up the street and turn to your right. . . . The Chimes? Yes, I agree. They do tug at your heart."

At the sign of triumph
Satan's host doth flee;
On, then, Christian soldiers,
On to victory!

The chimes are calling, and the people are coming as the music continues to peal forth from Shreveport's great downtown First Baptist Church.

This is the day the Lord hath made; His people are coming to His house to worship Him and hear God's man proclaim His message.

The great audience has gathered inside the portals, and you can feel the electricity of expectancy pulsating throughout the congregation. If you listen closely, you can hear the mixed feelings and thoughts of the people. This is a special day—Sunday, April 2, 1950; the people are observing their pastor's thirty-eighth and fiftieth anniversary—thirty-eight years as their pastor and fifty golden years as a preacher of the gospel.

A massive door is opening now—a door that seems even larger because of the elaborate framework which surrounds it—Dr. M. E. Dodd enters and ascends to his pulpit. His very entrance sends a hushed silence over the great body of people. Here is truly a man of God. The people realize that the ten-story tower that houses the chimes is not nearly as tall as this giant of the gospel who has just seated himself in his stately chair right behind his pulpit. His head is bowed heavily in his hand. The sweet aroma of bent-knee time from which he has just come is still so very fragrant.

He lifts his head and sees the mass of people, but in the midst of them he sees four words—We Would See Jesus. This inscription is tacked to the back of the magnificently carved pulpit, and with the position of his chair right behind this structure, he cannot look out at his congregation without seeing those words and feeling the great weight of responsibility that goes with them.

He prays, "Oh, Dear Lord, I know some have come to gaze and gape at me, but with your help, Father, we will let them see Jesus once again."

As he comes forward to begin his sermon, the faces before him lose their individuality and become one great field "white unto harvest." He speaks with vigor and clarity. The voice is ageless which always surprises many—for the voice does not match the age of the man—this fact making you more aware that he is being endowed with power from on high to preach this matchless gospel.

> The scripture this morning is found in 1 Corinthians 2:2: "For I determined not to know anything among you, save Jesus Christ, and Him crucified." This I used in the first sermon I ever preached fifty years ago. Times have changed, people have changed, but I see no need to change my text.

Oh, Christian, shouldn't this strengthen our faith? From horse and buggy, to the king of travel—the indescribable pieces of steel that literally fly on our highways—yet, God's Word is just as new, pungent, and fresh as ever before. What a gospel!

Whoa there! You cannot ring the chimes until you know what made them resound so far. Get out of your flying machine, and let us travel back to 1638. The conveyance we will ride in could not break a speed record, but the tempo of modern-day travel is subjected to such acceleration that this tortoise speed should be refreshing.

Daniel Dodd was the first member of the clan to venture across the Atlantic to the freedom-ringing shores of America. He settled at Bradford, Connecticut, where Yale University was founded. Many other Dodds, longing to worship their God in their own way, sought the shores of the New World and settled in Virginia, not far from Jamestown, shortly after John Smith had planted his colony.

The first Allen Dodd, great-great-great-grandfather of Monroe Elmon Dodd, further established the Dodd clan on the shores of America. As a wheelwright at that time, he was as vital to civilization as the automobile manufacturer today. On the wheels that Allen Dodd and his fellow craftsmen made, the settlers rolled back the wilderness and established a nation of freedom-loving people which we call God's country—the United States of America. Allen left a noble tradition to a family of sons, one of whom was named John. John, like his forefathers, was to follow the star of freedom westward into the Carolinas. Then there came into John's family the second Allen who crossed the Alleghenies with John Sevier to help found the state of Franklin, later to become the Volunteer state of Tennessee.

America entered the Era of Good Feelings, and James Monroe took over the helm of the federal government as president and established the golden text of the western hemisphere—the Monroe Doctrine. During this time the home of Allen Dodd II was blessed with a son. The parents decided he should bear the name of the great president, James Monroe.

James Monroe Dodd was the father of William Henry Dodd, who upheld the tradition of his family and demonstrated free enterprise in his home community. He acquired a farm at Brazil, Gibson County, Tennessee, ten miles from Trenton, the county seat. He was an industrious man and progressive in his thinking; therefore, he utilized the most modern equipment and methods. He was the first farmer of his community to acquire and operate a self-binding reaper for harvesting oats and wheat. He also operated a sorghum mill, a small lumber mill, and a wheat thresher.

William Henry's neighbor followed suit, and it was not long before all of Gibson County hummed with modern devices and became, by the Department of Agriculture's estimate, the second greatest agricultural county in the nation.

In 1878 Rutherford B. Hayes was president of our country, leading in the political realm. In the religious world, Charles Hadden Spurgeon was at his zenith, although his voice would soon cease to preach the marvelous gospel. Another giant, Dwight L. Moody, was making the world turn aside because he was determined to see what the Lord could do with "a man wholly consecrated to Him." As his life drew to a close, Moody wished he were twenty years younger. There was still so much to be done. But, his next thought was that God's work would not suffer. There would always be fresh workers as the old ones wore out.

Yes, the Lord raises up great men for each generation, and in the same year that these two men of God were growing more heavenward, there was born a son to William Henry and Lucy Williams Dodd on September 8, 1878, on a Sunday when the Word was being preached far and wide. This son was destined to proclaim the gospel to the uttermost parts of the world. What was this child's name? He didn't have one. Rural children of that time were not named immediately at birth. Such an important matter required much pondering and consultation among family and friends.

Naming a child *before* birth was also unheard of. Blessed events were just what the name implies and were not discussed publicly, or even within the family circle, prior to the arrival of the child. Many times children were many months old, or even one year, before a suitable name could be agreed upon. Often such children would be known as "Baby" or some other nickname — sometimes the nickname stuck and the intended name was lost to general usage. Therefore, the Dodd infant was quite a husky babe before his father did the honors of naming him Monroe for his father. Up to this time, many neighbors called him "No Name Dodd." The middle name Elmon was an invention; but, I think perhaps an inspired one — the Hebrew word "El" is a shortened form of the Hebrew word for "God," and the Latin "Mon" means world. Thus, Monroe Elmon Dodd was destined to preach a great God to a great world.

CHAPTER 2

Lickskillet

WHEN THE CIVIL WAR CAME TO A CLOSE, A SOUTHERN gentleman declared he was going to Brazil in South America so he could keep his slaves. He traveled as far as Lickskillet, Tennessee, and never went any farther. So they changed the town's name to Brazil after the place the man had so desired to go. In checking with the Gibson County seat in Trenton, they found no records about the name of Brazil originally. The registrar asked many of the old-timers—they said, "It was at one time known as Pin Hook and also as Lickskillet." Since Dr. Dodd always told the story of Lickskillet, so it shall be in this book. Perhaps Pin Hook could have been a nickname denoting the wonderful fishing on the riverbank at Big Creek.

Whether it was Pin Hook or Lickskillet, the name was changed to Brazil under the above stated circumstances, and Brazil was the name at the time Monroe Elmon Dodd was born. So, I had to know more about this particular spot. Just what did this speck of earth—Brazil, Tennessee—hold with memories of footprints now buried beneath the shifting sands? Could I uncover any of them? I just had to get my feet on the paths where Elmon had his beginnings. The urge grew to the point that I picked up the phone and asked for the pastor of the Poplar Grove Baptist Church in Brazil, Tennessee—this was the church that was so rich in the history of Dr. Dodd's beginnings. When I found out his name, I had to wait until he could find a telephone to use. Finally, he called, and our voices rose in high tones back and forth across the miles because the connection was barely audible. However, I understood enough to make plans to be at the weekly prayer meeting on Wednesday night at his church.

On Wednesday morning, April 30, 1955, at 6:00 A.M., my beloved mother and I left Shreveport on the trail for *The Chimes of Shreveport*. Brazil, Trenton, Jackson, and Memphis were the desired destinations. We arrived in Trenton around 6:00 P.M. that evening, pulled into a filling station and asked about hotel accommodations in Brazil. The attendant smiled real big and said, "Lady, there's no hotel in Brazil."

"Aren't there any rooms?" I asked.

"No, Ma'am."

"Well, where do people stay?" I asked exhaustedly.

"At the hotel here in Trenton—it's the only one!"

"Well, how do you get to Brazil?" I asked.

"Go down to church—next block, turn right—go second red light, turn left—be on 54 'til you come to first little store named Frog Jump—turn right on gravel road, go about six or seven miles 'til you come to Brazil."

We thanked him and drove to the hotel. My mind was still in a muddle over the directions—especially the Frog Jump. We registered at the little hotel, made a quick change and headed for Brazil, for it was growing dark now and the service would soon begin. We found the store named Frog Jump—turned off on the gravel road, and we were on our way. We watched the speedometer, and when we had gone around seven miles, I turned to Mother and said, "I'm afraid we've gone too far." Night was beginning to enfold us, but I noticed some gentlemen out on a porch and asked them how far it was to Brazil.

"This is it," they said.

"Where?" I cried.

"Right here, lady."

"Well, where's the Baptist Church?"

"Right up that path."

We had finally made it! And those dear folks received us with open arms—all friends and relatives of Elmon's. We were in the little Poplar Grove Church that had had so much meaning in the life of Dr. Dodd.

As I went to bed that night, I imagined that it was no longer 1955—Elmon was a boy once again. On the morrow I would see Brazil in the light of day.

As we made our way to Brazil again the next morning, there she was—the dirt roads, the combination stores with paths leading from them, and the homes of the people dotted around the countryside. Years had hardly disturbed the basic part of Brazil—it abounded with echoes! It could very well have looked the same when Elmon was a boy. The homes with the good old-fashioned hospitality like a breath of lavender and old lace, and the wood-burning stoves in the middle of the rooms resolved into their elements. The pure, undefiled simplicity was so refreshing. Everyone called him Elmon and spoke as if he had just left yesterday. Oh, the love in their eyes and voices—to them he was their dear friend and childhood playmate.

Then, in my mind's eye, I saw Elmon for the first time! He was five years old and was making his way with his father down to the banks of Big Creek. They were going fishing that morning, and the bare feet of the little boy were reaching for contact with the freshly scented earth.

"Elmon, you sit here on the bank, beneath these shady maples," said Papa Dodd, "and I'll be down here a ways. If you catch anything just holler."

How big Elmon felt—fishing all by himself with all his wonderful fishing equipment: a limb from a tree, a length of Coats spool cotton and a bent pin.

The author (above) visited M. F. Dodd's birthplace in Brazil (Lickskillet), Tennessee.

Burying his toes deeper into the dirt on the bank of Big Creek, he let the dust of silence settle far beyond the expectations of his five years, and sat dangling a worm in an unresponsive stream. His old tattered straw hat sat cocked on his head. Thatches of his hair played peek-a-boo through the holes. Then suddenly, piercing cries rang through trembling treetops.

"Come, Papa, come quick," screamed Elmon. "I've—I've caught a fish!"

Papa Dodd rushed to the boy's side to examine the prize.

"Where is your fish?"

"Here it is," said Elmon, as he held up a beautiful little perch—all of two inches long.

"Kinda small, don't you think, Son?"

"Well, I guess so, but I'm little too. But when I get bigger, I'm gonna catch a whopper!"

And in all the years ahead, no sport ever surpassed his love of fishing. The opportunities it afforded him would be a volume in itself. Many times he cast out his line and caught some whoppers, but as he drew the catch into the boat, he was victorious for the Lord. For as he fished with men, he was a

After reaching Dyersburg (above), Elmon jumped onboard a freight train bound for Paducah, Kentucky. The young runaway lasted about a week in the city and returned to Lickskillet tired and hungry.

fisher *of* men—many came to know the Lord when he preached his fishing sermon.

Elmon was a son of the soil, and the chores on the farm came naturally to him. Every rural child was expected to do his part, to be an economic asset rather than a liability. On cold, icy mornings with breath smoking in the frigid air, there were fires to build before warmth could come, wood waiting for the blade of the axe, and animals of all assortments giving out the familiar bucolic sounds that demanded feeding. There were wheat and oats to harvest, cotton to hoe and pick, fences to put up, and dozens of other endless tasks. He had all of this to do and as yet, there were very few modern inventions to lighten the load. All vehicles and implements were powered by horses, mules, and oxen. Clothes were all washed by hand. Wagons pulled by oxen labored slowly along the old Gibson County roads as these beasts of burden wearily drew loads of produce to and from market. Elmon was a driver of a three-yoke team of oxen, and he would haul lumber from his father's lumber mill.

Skyscrapers can never boast the ravenous beauty of the countryside—remote, rolling, and unvarnished—even the earth itself is alive. In the luscious brown dirt, the gold autumn leaves with touches of crimson, and the rich sunsets, God is there.

The rugged farm existence of Elmon's parents aged people before their time. They were born on the farm and lived their entire lives within a small rural area. Travel of any great distance was unknown. Amidst this quiet setting, the scion of an adventurous family tradition grew restless. One Sunday morning as Elmon stood looking across Forked Deer River with dreams of faraway lands in his eyes, the blood of his ancestral background welled within him. The world outside was beckoning—it was a very tempting finger to thirteen-year-old Elmon this particular morning. All of a sudden, the monstrous farm tasks became distasteful to him. It wasn't the labor, for he loved to work hard. But now these tasks were holding him as if leashed to one of the old poplar trees. He wanted to look beyond the horizon of his small world, down through the dim vista of coming years, but the farm was limiting him. That day, when Papa asked him to do something, he revolted at the parental discipline. Papa Dodd was a strict believer of the rule not to spare the rod. He applied it this morning. Now you must remember that Elmon was thirteen—practically a man. The fuzz on his upper lip had begun to turn dark and slightly coarse— this severe chastisement hurt his pride, and he rebelled against it.

"Papa shouldn't have done that," thought young Dodd, the turbulent, unappeasable emotions churning within him. He looked again across the rolling fields to yonder horizons and considered leaving. "Yes!" he said determinedly. "I *shall* leave home!"

He had no money and just a few clothes, but what difference did that make when before him lay adventure and freedom? Looking back upon Papa's broad acres for the last time, he ventured out into the unknown world—down a dusty road, Monroe Elmon Dodd trudged westward to the little town of Dyersburg.

While I was tracing the Dodd trail, Dyersburg became a must, so Mother and I made it our next stop. It was only twenty-eight miles to Dyersburg according to the sign we passed as our car sped down the highway through typical Tennessee countryside. "Twenty-eight miles," I mused. "Surely that child didn't walk twenty-eight miles." But then I realized that it probably wasn't that particular road because we had made the trip from Trenton and he from Brazil.

Upon arriving in Dyersburg—a very up-and-coming little city bustling with activity—I asked where the railroad station was and we made our way there. I ran into the ticket office breathlessly and asked the man behind the window, "How far is it from Brazil to Dyersburg if I were walking down a dusty road through the mountains?" Looking rather puzzled, he said, "Lady, you're not planning to walk it, are you?"

"Oh no!" I cried and explained my mission.

"It would be a good twenty miles—even with a shortcut."

So Elmon had walked twenty miles to catch a train. I could almost hear the rhythmic clacking of the train wheels on the antiquated streak of silver just outside the station and asked the question, "Is that the same track that was here in 1891?"

"Yes, this is the only station in town and the only one that has ever been here."

I then went out to look up and down the track with an inexpressible feeling of expectancy—I turned my head just in time to catch a vision of Elmon climbing aboard a freight train rolling northward toward the great metropolis of Paducah, Kentucky.

It wasn't long before hunger pains became very real to the runaway. A friendly brakeman, sensing the boy's condition shared his cold ham sandwich which was quite a feast for such a hungry boy.

The bustle of city traffic in Paducah was strange to ears which were tuned to chirping crickets of the rural countryside. Ah, this was a new world! Things which he had heard of, but not seen. He looked with eager eyes upon the amazing scenes of city life—never dreaming that he would one day be the pastor of the First Baptist Church in the city of his first travels. After a week, his bumptious spirit was wearing thin with a pang striking close to his vital organs that spoke of another sort of hunger—his old self-reliance was gone! So, he returned to Brazil, realizing that home and Mama's cooking were pretty nice.

He didn't go straight to the house though, but stopped to play baseball with the other boys, as well as build up his courage to face Papa.

He was just coming into homeplate when Mama and Papa happened by. Miss Lucy pleaded with Papa in her benign way to stop so she could see her boy, but Papa wouldn't stop; he just made the horses giddyap, and go faster. "He will come home when he's ready," he said.

As I left the train tracks at Dyersburg, I thought of how this adventure into the outside world was only the beginning of globe-trotting for M. E. Dodd the pioneer. Back at the car, Mother asked, "What did you find?"

"A runaway feasting on a cold ham sandwich, and now I'm hungry!"

So, we went to the hotel and ate. While we were dining, I asked the waitress where Forked Deer River was. I wanted to see the river towards which Monroe Elmon had directed his gaze that faraway Sunday morning.

"I never heard of it," she said.

Elmon was a dreamer as a young boy, and the Forked Deer River, shown above, seemed to beckon him to leave the farm. At the age of thirteen, he set out for Dyersburg, Tennessee, seeking adventure.

"But it's right around here, you must have heard of it."

"Maybe you mean Fork-ed Deer River," she said.

I had pronounced it as one syllable, like I had forked something with a fork.

The waitress pronounced it "Fork-ed." After dinner, we hurriedly left to have a look at the Forked Deer River. After going a few blocks and crossing the railroad track, we found ourselves on a bridge with the river on either side. I got out and looked in all directions.

As far as the eye could see there were tall trees clothed in black, reaching toward the heavens with long spidery arms. They stood in the middle of the stream and along the banks. As the water lapped at the trunks, I thought of the tree of life and the water of which we will never thirst. Yes, trees were barren of their crowning glory, yet somehow stately, midst the murky water—its musical voice resonating through a throat of sand—narrating Elmon's first great adventure.

CHAPTER 3

Matchless Music

NEWSPAPERS REVEAL HISTORY, AND I WAS MOST ANXIOUS TO find some old copies in Trenton. I was told there were two newspaper offices. One informed me that their early back issues had been destroyed by fire. With a heavy heart, I went to the *Herald Register* seeking dates and facts, but never anticipated the feeling of stepping back into the past which I experienced when the editor, Richard E. Davis, came forward to greet me. Finding it difficult to catch my breath, I asked, "Did anyone ever tell you how much you resemble Dr. M. E. Dodd?"

"Yes," he smiled, "Everyone!"

Editor Davis had papers dating back to 1900; even with the weekly paper coming off the press, the whole staff pitched in to help me secure the news I needed for my story. Hearsay was narrowed down to the actual facts. The old *Herald Democrat* (name of the paper in the early 1900s) came alive—they were making my "rough recital" aptly chime.

Before I made my departure from the *Herald Register*, Mr. Davis found a copy of *Gibson County Tenn*[essee]—an illustrated history and progress edited and compiled by W. P. Greene. It was an old book with a wonderful biographical sketch of William Henry Dodd along with a photograph of the patrician gentleman. My mother, who had become a faithful traveling companion for the trip, was sitting nearby hanging on to every word as I began to read about Papa Dodd:

> He was the son of James Monroe and Pricilla Perry Dodd and was born in the Sixth District of Gibson County Tennessee on March 16, 1851—the Civil War coming on. . . . When he was only ten, and the responsibility of the farm falling on him as the oldest son. He did not enjoy the advantages of an early school education. Like thousands of other sons of our Southern

heroes, he had to give all his time to the support of the family, while the father did service on the battlefield, but along the educational line a sufficient height was attained by close individual study to make successes of his ventures and to accomplish all that an ambitious mind led him to undertake. On May 17, 1877, he was married to Mrs. Lucy Strong, daughter of Capt. T. W. Williams and to them were born four children — Elmon, Allen, Robert, and Annie, (Lucy had three sons by her former marriage).

When married, Mr. Dodd settled on a farm near Brazil in the Fifth District of the County where he resided until 1899 when he moved with his family to Trenton for the purpose of giving the children better educational advantages. While on the farm, he devoted his time to stock raising especially and farming in general. In the year 1892, he engaged in the manufacture of lumber with Mr. W. T. Ingram under the firm name of Ingram and Dodd. The success of this business was encouraging enough to induce him to purchase Mr. Ingram's interest in the mills in 1898. William Henry had a natural love for mathematics and in 1897 became deeply interested in the science of surveying and at once obtained instruments and books for the study of the same. By individual efforts he acquired a proficiency in this art, and was solicited to accept a deputyship under County Surveyor L. W. Morgan. He did so and met with much encouragement in this work. At the January 1901 term of the county court he was elected for a 4 year term of office of County Surveyor.

And how did the people of the early 1900s feel about him?

Mr. Dodd is a most exemplary and upright citizen, esteemed for his noble qualities of heart and mind by his intimate friends and popular with the general public for his obliging disposition and strict devotion to his public duties.

Before the family moved to Trenton, foundations were laid which cannot be rivaled. August 12, 1892 in Brazil, Tennessee, found young Elmon plowing in his father's fields. The heat of the day was already bearing down on his thirteen-year-old back, making his haven of an old poplar tree look very enticing. There was to be no respite this day from sun that melts and fatigues. The heat, however, was barely noticed by the lad because of the burning sensation in his heart. Three nights before he had joined his friends in a pilfering raid upon a neighbor's watermelon patch. Although many considered it lightly as just another boyhood prank, Elmon's heart was heavy as his conscience kept pricking him, and he realized he was weighted down by the conviction of sin upon his soul. The plowing done, young Dodd made his way toward the house. But before he reached his mother's door, he was drawn to his trysting place, an old poplar stump. Clinging to it, he poured out words of remorse to his heavenly Father.

As he prayed, he thought of dear old deacon Sam Benge, a six-foot-two-inch farmer with sandy hair and a florid face; the first man to ever tell him his salvation was a matter of prayer. "Somebody thinks enough of me to pray for me," he thought. Evening found him walking the mile and a half to the Poplar Grove Baptist Church where a revival was in progress. Suddenly a great light flashed upon his soul, and he knelt beside a poplar tree on the roadside and began to pray.

> Oh come, come, come, come, come
> to the church in the wildwood.
> Oh come to the church in the dale . . .

The music reached out and drew a young boy into the church pew. Forest Smith, a student at Union University was preaching that evening, and he called on the penitent ones to come and accept Christ. Elmon Dodd took a step, then hesitated. "Don't go," said the devil, "Your little sins won't be near as much fun with Jesus in your heart."

Ronnie McClaren, one of Elmon's chums standing nearby, saw the momentary struggle and went over to him. "Elmon," pleaded this whole-hearted son of the soil, "Don't you want to go forward?"

Elmon, his soul aflame with emotion, strode down the aisle. In reflecting upon the greatest occasion that can ever happen in anyone's life, Dr. Dodd said of his own experience, "I gave the preacher my hand, my heart to God, and my life to the church." And of his crystalline conversion upon the roadside that night, he said, "I felt the touch of the kindest hand that was ever laid upon a troubled boy's shoulder. It was the nail-scarred hands of Calvary. There I saw the sweetest face upon which eyes ever gazed. Yea, the face of the Son of God! Then I heard the most matchless music that ever sounded in human ears: 'Thy sins be forgiven thee!' Thus, I yielded my whole heart in undying devotion to Jesus Christ as Savior and Lord."

"Tell the joyful tidings, bear it far away! For a precious soul is born again. Glory! Glory! How the loud harps ring." Yes, ring the bells of heaven, there was joy that day when the Father met Elmon out upon the way, welcoming His weary wandering child.

Nothing else would satisfy me now but to make my way out to what was left of the old home place. An old barn and the poplar trees were all that remained. I saw an old stump which could very easily have been the one where Elmon poured out his heart. Then, I walked down the dusty road which his feet had trod that evening on the way to the Poplar Grove Baptist Church. The original site of the church was just an open field, but I stood in the middle of it with twilight fast approaching and a welcome breeze sweeping the high sun-parched grass up around my ankles. I bowed my head and thanked the Lord for all the special fields where He has met His children, and especially for this one!

After being accepted into Poplar Grove, Elmon took his membership seriously. The open church doors found him there with numerous opportunities to serve. When Elmon had been a Christian only a year, the fourteen-year-old lad attended a church conference at which a typical Baptist discussion was forthcoming. Wrinkles were showing in the old church. Paint and repairs were a must. However, times were not prosperous, and money was scarce. Among the rural folk of the flock, the matter of raising the money had baffled even the pillars of the faith.

Monroe Elmon Dodd rose timidly and with a dauntless spirit asked that he be permitted to raise the necessary funds. Though doubtful what the boy could do, it was the best suggestion any member—young or old—had presented. The deacons and members readily agreed. Monday found the Brazil countryside dotted with a little pony ridden by Elmon. They scurried along, stopping at every farmhouse, making an earnest plea for the dear old Poplar Grove. His sincere appeal found the hands of women reaching into sugar bowls and old stockings—savings from their egg money.

The men in the fields, not to be outdone, mopped sweated brows and dug down into pockets of hard-earned money; sometimes a dollar found its way into the collection, but for the most part, it was small change. The following Saturday, Elmon strode into the church and proudly presented the collection to his elders. With a few more contributions from those gathered, there was enough to paint and repair the beloved old church. And down through the years when Southern Baptists needed a leader who could get the people to give of their income, they chose none other than M. E. Dodd.

From numerous experiences dealing with the value of money and how to raise it for the service of the Lord, Dr. Dodd coined this proverb: "An ounce of energy, a pound of talent, an hour of time, a dollar of money given to the church will go farther, rise higher, sink deeper, spread wider, last longer, and accomplish more than when given to any other cause in the world."

In the *Baptist Message* following a special article on the life of Dr. Dodd, Udell Smith, state BSU Secretary for Louisiana, recalled an event during his own boyhood.

> The depression was in its final throes and our family was in typical financial straits. My father and I attended the First Baptist Church of Shreveport one Sunday evening and heard the Louisiana Baptist Children's Home choir sing. Dr. Dodd urged the congregation to give generously to the Children's Home. My father had $1.26 which had to last at least two more days. When the offering plate was passed, he gave the $ .26. Later in the service, Dr. Dodd announced that the offering was not quite enough and the plates would be passed again. He made such an urgent plea that my father gave his last dollar. When we left the service, Dad quipped, "I must quit coming to hear that crazy Dodd preach. I simply can't afford it!"

Before we leave Brazil and surrounding area, come with me as we go from house to house and visit Elmon's childhood friends. One sweet home that walked right out of yesterday was that of Miss Emma Dew. The potbellied stove in the middle of the room and other trappings were so in keeping with another day that I expected Elmon to walk in any minute.

"We all called him Elmon," she said, "and loved, and looked up to him. He was older than some of us, and as time went by, we called him Mr. Dodd." Then her eyes misted, "Allen, Dr. Dodd's younger brother, was my sweetheart. I still have a little silver thimble that he gave me." She walked over to the shelf where the thimble sat and brought it to me. I could tell this was a sacred object to her, and I handled it in like manner. "I never married!" she said.

Bess Taylor Anthony, a cousin of Elmon's was not at home, but wrote later, "I loved Elmon very much — when my husband and I were living in Paducah, we went to his church on a Sunday night to hear him preach and were very impressed by the crowds he would draw, even on Sunday nights. Elmon was a great person — so kind and understanding. What I remember most about him was his joy in being a Christian — no sad, long-faced preacher!" This was quite a feat, I thought; because, these were the days of cutaway coats and a pompous air of piety. "But make no mistake about it," she went on, "Emma was always in there pitching, so she must share credit in all he did after they were married."

Ahhhh, strains of Emma, I mused. Wherever I looked, she was always by his side. All the places we visited, the song was still the same. "Dr. Elmon," some called him lovingly. Even though he became a world citizen for the cause of Christ, that speck of earth and the inhabitants thereof always claimed him as their first citizen!

Chapter 4

A Call
Comes Ringing

MISS LUCY, THE TITLE WHICH PAPA DODD FONDLY GAVE Mama Dodd, was a Primitive Baptist. She would go to her footwashing the first Sunday in May, the regular day for this event. She wanted Elmon to be a preacher and much time was spent in prayer that the Heavenly Father would call him, but she didn't believe in educating to the ministry. Miss Lucy believed in predestination and said to Elmon, "Son, if I believed the way you do, I would walk these streets day and night!"

Papa Dodd's strength of character, fine spirit, and belief in God would withstand the sands of time like sea breakers beating against the rocks that would not waver; yet, this stalwart gentleman was not a Christian and did not accept Christ until several years after his son had been preaching. The *Baptist Review* of December 1947 reads: "Dr. Dodd was a young pastor at Fulton, Kentucky, and had written his first tract — *Safe if Saved*. It occurred to him, 'Here I am trying to win others to Christ, and I have not even convinced my own father of his need for Christ.'" He sat down and sent his father the first tract he had ever written. Within a week, he had a letter from his father asking him to come and baptize him. Dr. Dodd made the trip back to the old home church and baptized the elder Dodd in a nearby creek at the insistence of his father, even though the church had a baptistry.

Elmon was always a leader in all school activities, especially athletic, literary, and oratorical contests. At the age of fourteen, he represented his school and was the victor in one of the ten famous "Demerits Prohibition Contests" winning a silver medal.

He broke his school training and entered the classroom as a teacher at the age of seventeen and taught one session. It was there in the schoolroom that he began to study and gain insight into human nature, which through the years enabled him to know men with a great degree of certainty. Monroe

Elmon Dodd was a seventh-generation American via Virginia, the Carolinas, and Tennessee. His ancestors came from Cheshire on the border of Wales and have followed the national colors in every American fight for freedom. Many of his ancestors took part in famous battles that would make any true red, white, and blue heart beat a little faster. Many were illustrious heroes of the wars, winning honors on fields of battle. However, space does not permit this interesting lineage of battle participation, but just this brief background for a young man who came along and upheld the family tradition in two great wars.

On a sunny April 8, 1898, Elmon was plowing on the farm near Brazil. With the Spanish-American War in the forefront, Elmon Dodd, the progeny of great hearts in the fight for freedom, felt strongly the passion to respond to the call for volunteers in what was to be the last and only entirely volunteer wartime army in the history of the nation. So nineteen-year-old Elmon left home again and went by bicycle into Trenton the next day, where he joined Company K of the Second Tennessee Volunteers. His commanding officer was Captain Quentin Rankin, who, along with Colonel R. E. Taylor, was a victim of the Reelfoot Lake Lynching, one of the bloodiest tragedies in Tennessee history. (A few hours before the lynching party arrived, William Henry Dodd, Elmon's father, who had been a member of Rankin's surveying party, departed from the camp. Had he remained, his fate could very easily have been the same as Captain Rankin's or Colonel Taylor's.) Company K boarded the train for Nashville, and Elmon, with a backward glance at the Gibson County countryside, joined his commander as the train carried him farther from home on his way to training grounds.

One of young Dodd's first duties was to guard the command tent of Major Sevier. Inside was a strange looking mechanism he was told was a telephone. "And when it rings answer it," his superior commanded as he was left on guard one night. He walked his post in the darkness, back and forth as soldierly as his body could be with terrifying thoughts of the telephone in his mind. Fresh from the plow, a young country boy who had never talked on a phone or seen Mr. Bell's invention, he walked his post praying that the thing would not ring. It became an instrument of torture. As he left duty the next morning, he sighed with relief. His prayer had been answered.

Leaving Nashville, the Second Tennessee Volunteer went to Washington, and on his first leave, he went sightseeing just like any other soldier. At one place, they were having a display of a flying machine. It was an odd contraption made of canvas, bicycle wheels, and an engine. It made quite an impression on him, as he idly imagined himself flying through the blue, little dreaming that one day he would be called "the flying parson." As he left the flying machine, he wondered if maybe it could go as far as Brazil;

tinges of homesickness were beginning to come over him. He then visited the Washington Monument and went to the top of the 555-foot memorial. That evening, as he wrote to the folks at home, he said, "I could see every place but home." No, he couldn't see home, and he couldn't yet see the Almighty Hand that was beckoning mighty hard for him to come follow Him and be a soldier of the Cross.

Upholding family tradition, one of the last things that young Elmon Dodd did as a soldier was to scribble on a scrap of paper: *To the next boy who gets this gun, May the Lord have mercy on your soul. Signed, Monroe Elmon Dodd.* Then he tucked it into the barrel of his old Springfield rifle just before it was turned in at his discharge. Thirty years later, an old Springfield rifle was sold in a store in Memphis and the buyer, a man named Pickard, found Elmon Dodd's note. He gave it to the *Memphis News Scimitar*, which headlined a feature story: "Homesick soldier bequeaths his gun to successor with a blessing."

If that note Elmon penned had been probed a little deeper, we would find more than just a homesick boy. "May the Lord have mercy on your soul" suggests that the Lord was beginning to come through to him, and he was beginning to have a greater concern for the souls of men.

The studying of his Bible in a more serious vein came about while soldiering in the Spanish-American War. He found the army camp a good place to study the Bible, and as questions were asked when he read aloud to others, he found it was also a splendid place for scattering seeds in behalf of the cause of Christ. Yes, a ringing in his ears was becoming clearer. He was mustered out in February 1899, in Columbia, South Carolina, and he was on his way home from a war that marked the emergence of the United States as a world power. The Lord had been very close to him during the war, and he now knew that He was calling him to preach, but he was resisting it because a career as a lawyer was first and foremost. The threads of education which had been broken were picked up again with renewed fervor. So much time had already been lost.

He enrolled in Peabody High School in Trenton, and . . . well, just let me take you there for a moment. "Is this the same building that Dr. Dodd went to," I asked. "No," they answered, "but, it is the same site." I had to go outdoors then and walk across the ground to a huge tree on the campus. Yes, I thought, he could very easily have sat underneath these branches as his dreams were beginning to take wings. I sat down and closed my eyes trying to visualize the young people of 1899 at old Peabody. As I daydreamed, Elmon came walking briskly across the campus.

"Hello," I called. "Where are you going?"

"I've just come from an elocution lesson. I could stay there all day."

"Yes," I said, "your beaming face shows you've just come from a great love."

"Yes, it does mean a lot to me," he said, "and if I can speak at all I owe more than I even know to my expression teacher."

Then he was gone as quickly as he had come. I strolled back into the building—it was very much 1955—the halls were alive with waves of sound that belonged to teenage voices. I then went to the classroom of Mrs. Bond Skakeford Hargrove, a teacher who had been a classmate of Elmon's at Peabody. Her eyes took on a gleam as she talked. "I never saw him do anything ungentlemanly," she said. "Everybody called him, Mr. Dodd, because he was so much older than we were. We teased him, but we respected him. Everything he did he had to do."

Later, I went to see Mattie Wright (Mrs. Harry) Elder who had been Elmon's girlfriend in high school. As she opened the door, I fell in love right away with that dainty lady with silver hair and piercing eyes. The very essence of true Southern hospitality, she served us tea out of delicate little china cups. "Yes," her eyes twinkled, "I knew Elmon. He was a normal boy and very mischievous, full of fun and not an angel. When he was going to school at Brazil, my father was the schoolmaster." Mattie continued, "Father was very strict and made Elmon tow the mark. He and another boy vowed when they were grown they were going to whip him."

"What do you think made him *tick*, Mrs. Elder?"

"His perseverance had created an indomitable spirit. He had his aim high, and he never stopped until he reached it."

As I was taking my leave, she added, "So much credit goes to Mrs. Dodd. He married the right one for him." That phrase was repeated over and over again.

The field of law was ever beckoning; yet at times, visions of law books turned into books of law from the Bible. God was calling him to preach and he was beginning to feel, "Woe is me, if I preach not the gospel."

As Elmon walked into the house, October 7, 1899, Mama Dodd met him at the door. "Allen took sick real sudden," her voice quivered. "It's bilious colic, I believe." Allen was two years younger than Elmon and had surrendered to be a Methodist minister. Elmon strode quickly to his brother's bedside, sensing something more serious than Mama had told him. Elmon tried to conceal his feelings upon seeing the drawn face of his brother that had been bright and smiling just hours earlier.

"Don't try to talk, Allen; conserve your strength so you can get well."

"No, Elmon, I've got to say this, Brother," he gasped feebly, "God called both of us to preach . . . you have . . . and now I am dying. Won't you answer that call, and while doing your work as a minister, do a bit for me too?"

Years later, when Dr. Dodd was a great preacher, people would remark about his driving energy—a drive that at times seemed impossible for a human to have and survive. In response to them, he would tell about the request of his brother and quietly explain, "That's why I work sixteen hours a day—eight hours for myself and eight hours for my brother."

Does a call come ringing with the appearance of the death angel? Eternity alone will tell. But, when his brother summoned him to preach and "do" some for him, his mind was settled. "If God wants me to preach— I will!"

He preached his first sermon on April 8, 1900, while a high school student in Trenton. Some of his fellow students went to Poplar Grove to hear his first sermon. Among them were Hillsman Taylor, Ben Taylor, and Mamie Bowers. I talked to them about their first impression of Dr. Dodd's preaching.

"I knew then he was going places, he just had something."

"When I drove out on a dusty dirt road to hear Elmon preach, I'm afraid my mind was more on the boy beside me than the sermon I was to hear that day. However, I enjoyed the sermon, and was proud he could preach such a good one. Even then, he had a good voice—one that grew so warm and mellow. I was just in high school, but I followed his career with great pride."

Yes, his young friends were just a group of typical teenagers going to stand by their friend, not realizing this was a neophyte work—the beginning of a great pioneer for God.

And what did the *Trenton Herald Democrat* of April 13, 1900, have to say? "From Brazil—quite a large crowd assembled at the Baptist church last Sunday to hear Rev. Elmon Dodd deliver his initiatory sermon."

His efforts exceeded the most sanguine expectations of his numerous friends. One said, "Elmon was reared among us, and we feel justly proud of him as a neighbor boy. Would that we had more devoted Christian young men, for the laurels won by a consecrated life are more to be appreciated than those won by the hero of Manila."

Oddly enough, the headlines of this same paper read: "The Secret of Success is Keeping Everlastingly At It."

Then I wanted to go once more to the birthplace and see the ground Elmon had trod as a child. The countryside was streaked with a furious conference of livid pink from a splendid sunset. We arrived in Brazil that evening and two of Elmon's playmates, Miss Emma Dew and Kate Benge Davis, who had known him as a little boy, took us to the small Presbyterian cemetery where we gazed tenderly at tomb headpieces reading *James Monroe, Precilla Perry Wade, William Henry, Lucy Ann Williams, Allen Benjamin.* "Allen was my sweetheart," Miss Emma said again, as she wiped a tear from her eye—one that was just as fresh as if he had just gone yesterday. Kate spoke up, "It was my father, Sam Benge, that spoke to Elmon about becoming a Christian."

The years 1847–1924 appeared on Miss Lucy's tombstone. They told me that it was one of the great joys of his mother's life that she lived until the coming of radio and for many months was able to hear her beloved son as she sat in her Tennessee home. Papa Dodd lived to the age of ninety-seven; he was living with his son at the time of his death.

As we rambled along the paths he had trod, I thought of Elmon's younger years. The early days of his life were spent on the farm of old Tennessee. He has never forgotten the happy experience and the tender ministrations of his parents. Even now, with all the cares and responsibilities of a great downtown church, together with the multiplied hundreds of denominational and extra-denominational demands, he finds time to go as a pilgrim, twice each year, to the haunts of his childhood.

There, amidst the scenes which indelibly impressed him years ago, his spirit and soul seem to be recharged; his whole life sweetened and deepened by the flood-tide of remembrances. He comes away better and bigger of heart, more determined in spirit and resolute in purpose to carry forward with renewed zeal the work of Christ's kingdom.

Pensively I mused, as I knelt at Elmon's old trysting place—the old stump at the back of the house—I had discovered another of the secrets of his life. I suppose that's why we must all go back once in a while to the particular earth we came from—to find ourselves again. *It was this special earth where I found Elmon again. The grounds seemed to bow to his memory, and the whirls of dust whispered his name.*

CHAPTER 5

Room
Fifty-three

HIS PARENTS FINALLY CAME TO HIS WAY OF THINKING regarding his chosen vocation, but the beginnings were not easy. One of Elmon's close friends of his youthful years stated, "His father was very well to do and quite an extensive landowner. His father told him if he would give up preaching, he would send him to Harvard University. However, with a stubborn, determined streak full of conviction, Elmon refused this offer and the elder Dodd, equally determined, refused Elmon any assistance towards his religious education. With this exhortation from Papa Dodd, and Mama not believing in educating to the ministry, young Dodd gathered his credits together from Peabody High School and left home for Jackson, Tennessee, twenty-eight miles from Trenton, the home of Union University.

There in the fall of 1900, he began his education for the gospel ministry, staying in Adams Hall on the campus grounds, doing odd jobs to pay his tuition. The strain at home had not eased, and it wasn't long before his freshman year was interrupted because of ill health. For two months, he recuperated with relatives in Missouri who had everything that was needed to minister to this preacher boy. His health soon regained, the young student, full of zeal and enthusiasm, anxiously returned to his studies at Union.

As he made his way back to the university on the train, a young man came in and sat beside him. Elmon thought—I wonder if he is a Christian? "Oh, I'm sure he is," he said to himself, and continued reading a most absorbing book in which he was engrossed. "But perhaps I should speak to him. After all, it is my place. I have been called of God to proclaim the gospel to everyone." Then that spirit of procrastination which tempts so many of us said to him, "Oh, finish your book; you have plenty of time to speak to this fellow. His soul can wait and besides, why embarrass yourself—he's probably already a Christian."

In a very few minutes, the train came to a sudden stop, the young man at Dodd's side left his seat and alighted from the train. Elmon Dodd's eyes followed him as he joined a group of men at the station. He watched as they passed the bottle of liquid made in hell. Ribald stories and oaths followed. He heard the young man he had wanted to speak to take the Lord's name in vain. He knew now he was not a Christian.

The wheels began to move as the whistle blew and the clanging of the bell burst his eardrum as they rang, "You've missed an opportunity, you've missed an opportunity." "Yes," he cried, "a golden opportunity. As an evangelist of the Lord, I have failed." He dropped to his knees with the arrows of sorrow striking his heart, and begged God's forgiveness. He made a vow right there that he would never again neglect an opportunity to tell the unsaved of salvation through Christ—be it one person or a great host. This was a vow he kept until God called him home.

It was Saturday and Elmon's spirits were very low as he left the campus of Union University to fill the pulpit at Cooper's Chapel Baptist Church. Financial problems loomed before him that seemed as tightly drawn as prison bars. "Behind with my board and tuition; even with my odd jobs, it's just not enough," he thought. With burdened heart and worried frame of mind, he stepped off the train as it stopped at the little station. The chilling winds were blowing mercilessly, and a fresh zephyr came and played a xylophone interlude on his spinal column. Elmon drew his overcoat closer and higher trying to guard off the bitter wind. He glanced around the seemingly deserted station to find the conveyance that was to take him several miles farther to the church. There was a farm mule accompanied by a twelve-year-old boy on another mule—the two mules and the boy were also shivering in the cold. Mounted upon this spiritless and forlorn creature, the student pastor found more misery in store; the mule's trot shook him terribly as the wind froze him to the bone. Tired and weary, he and his companion arrived at the farmhouse where he was to spend the night. The rugged journey had not helped the melancholy mood and the darkened moroseness that had prevailed since he left the campus.

The following day was even more trying. Only a handful of members of the little church braved the weather to attend services. "It seems like they could have made more of an effort," thought the young minister. "I braved the elements to come to them—surely they could have shown a little more loyalty." A service followed which lacked zeal or spirit on the part of anyone. Elmon had hopes that the collection would be enough to pay his college dues. The total was turned over to the pastor and the contents was only a trickle of small change. When counted, the aggregate amount wasn't even enough to pay his train fare. This was the end—he just couldn't take anymore.

A wave of despondency enveloped Elmon as he made his way back to Adam's Hall at Union University that night. As he entered room fifty-three, lines of discouragement marked his young face; turning to his roommate Warren Hill, Elmon Dodd came forth with an outburst from his harnessed emotions, "Why the ministry? It's not a career! I'm not a traveler on a theological road—a rash of ritual . . . the pressure of the ecclesiastical yoke—I'm through!" With that, he hurled his Bible to the floor, "I'm through, I'm through, I can't take anymore," he shouted. Anger and despair were playing havoc with his heart, but the disapproving eyes of his roommate were more vehement than Elmon's outburst. Warren went over to Elmon and put his arm around his heaving shoulders, gently but firmly reproving him. The passion of the moment subsided, and he was filled with shame and remorse. He fell to his knees and picked up his Bible with tender care. "God forgive me," he murmured. Then he opened the one and only book and still on his knees (a custom he followed always thereafter), he read from the Twenty-third Psalm. "The Lord is my Shepherd, I shall not want," a sweet moistness filled the young minister's eyes as he devoured those precious words. Then he promised that never again would he let the desire for material things interfere with the Lord's work. "I will be a citadel of the Spirit," he declared, and he never went back on this promise. Why, he thought, didn't I endure cold and privations for this country during the Spanish-American War? Why not as much for God? These decisions made in youth were forming a power for the Lord of which he was not aware.

Monday morning, Elmon resumed his studies with renewed faith and a stalwart heart, although his financial problems still loomed like pools of shadows. He waited on tables and collected laundry with greater enthusiasm. The next day, he went to the post office looking for a letter from his best girl. There was a letter, but from another source. It was a large, well-stuffed envelope postmarked from the little settlement where he had preached the Sunday before. Hurriedly, he opened it, and out dropped a roll of money. Eagerly, Elmon read the note that accompanied the money.

Dear Brother Dodd,
I was too ill and it was too cold for me at my age to attend services at Cooper's Chapel on Sunday. I was praying Sunday night and received an impression that you needed money. Take this gift from me, and may God bless you.

The letter was signed by an elderly woman—the only member of any means in that little flock. Elmon dropped to his knees and poured out his heart, full of thanks to a merciful heavenly Father who answers prayer; the roll contained enough money to pay all his obligations with some left over. On his next visit to Cooper's Chapel, young Dodd learned that the good woman had written the letter at the exact moment he had cried out, "I'm quitting!" and fell on his knees to beg God's forgiveness for such an outburst. We kneel in weakness, we arise full of power, yet we deny ourselves this privilege because we have not taken time to tap this tower of strength and ring the bell of prayer.

One day during Elmon's first year at Union, several ministerial students engaged a wagon and team to take them to a country church for a Fifth Sunday Meeting. The cost was one dollar, but Elmon didn't have the dollar. V. Franklin Ray, a senior student saw the need and was a friend indeed — he put the dollar in for him. Elmon Dodd read the Scripture and led in prayer at the meeting — it was the first public part in a denominational meeting. The dollar that was loaned him that day resulted in a beautiful story. Years later when Dr. Dodd was president of a college which bore his name, he received a letter from V. Franklin Ray, who was a missionary to Japan. Dr. Ray was inquiring about Dodd College as a prospective school for his daughter. Dr. Dodd called Ray saying, "Send your daughter, there will be no charge to you. I've been owing you a dollar with compound interest for years." Miss Ray came.

We never know the reach of the earth in which we sow a seed. It was at Union that he had the opportunity of becoming closely associated with Dr. G. M. Savage, the beloved president, and professors H. C. Erby, C. S. Young, A. M. Wilson, and R. V. Dupree. They were godly men who made their contribution to his life and character.

Still on our pilgrimage of the young Monroe Elmon Dodd, I left Trenton and headed for Jackson and Union University. When Mother and I arrived, the daylight hours had been taken from us. With much reluctance, I had to await the dawn of a new day. Excited sleep followed. I wondered if Adams Hall would still be there.

Through all of his university life, he was an outstanding leader in all the activities of the student body. He won practically every medal and prize offered for debate, declamation, and literary contents. He was given the Strickland Medal for Oratory — this medal was awarded until 1996. He was editor-in-chief of the college magazine, which under his leadership became one of the leading college magazines of the South. He named the college annual *Lest We Forget* and was honored by the student body by being elected literary editor of that publication. He assisted in the first edition of the annual and was instrumental with the assistance of the other members of the editorial staff in laying the foundation for its future. *Lest We Forget* holds a tender place in the hearts of many alumni and the annual still bears the same name to this day.

Dr. George Martin Savage, president of Union University, admired the young aspiring preachers, and even with his austerity was revered by all his students. He would take them as boarders in his home and let them do work around the house to help with their tuition. Elmon Dodd was privileged to stay in the president's home along with other students. Elmon felt the warmth of his imposing personality and came under the kind influence of this great man. Many wonderful servants of God have come from those who knew Dr. Savage; after all, that is a man's real monument—the investments he has made in the lives of young people by spiritual leadership.

The Savage home that had meant so much in the life of Monroe Dodd—I wondered if it was still standing. Even Mrs. Dodd wasn't sure whether it was or not.

A new day found me at Union. As I made my way across the wooded campus, I stopped two young men on their way to class, "Could you tell me if you have an Adams Hall?"

"Yes, just behind you," they said. So it was still there, but was it the same one that had housed Elmon's heartaches?

In a few moments I was being ushered into President Warren F. Jones's office. As I took his hand, I was conscious of an aristocrat of the highest quality.

"Dr. Jones," I asked, "would that be the same Adams Hall that was here when Dr. Dodd was a student?"

"I am not sure," he said, "But we will find out." A call revealed that the east wing of Adams Hall was still the same, the oldest wing on the campus. The other part was destroyed by fire in 1918.

"Is Dr. Savage's home still here?"

"Oh yes," he said, "Right across the street from Adams Hall at 604 East College Street. The Savage name is a magical word here. Also we have an M. E. Dodd award," Dr. Jones continued, "for expository writing. Ministerial students prepare an expository sermon, then they expound. The award is a set of lovely commentaries."

"Would it be possible," I asked, "To see some of the back volumes of the college annual?"

"Yes, indeed," answered Dr. Jones. "Let me call the librarian so she will be expecting you. Also, have you seen Dr. Ray? He knew Dr. Dodd as a young man."

"What a streak of luck," I responded, "to find him here."

A wave of nostalgia crept over me in the library as I went through early editions of *Lest We Forget*; I felt like a coed of the early 1900s.

I found Dr. Ray just as he was getting ready to leave his house, but for this mission he could wait. A missionary to Japan from 1901–1912, he had that "singing in the rain" missionary zeal that made you want to literally sit at his feet and listen to every word.

"Do you remember that dollar you loaned Dr. Dodd when you were students?" I asked.

With twinkling eyes, he emphatically said, "I invested that dollar in Dr. Dodd. . . . Ah yes," he continued in a state of reminiscence. "Dr. Dodd was a wonderful preacher of the Word of God and a great friend of preachers and especially of missionaries."

"Yes," I thought as I left Dr. Ray. "Missionaries all over the world would second that last statement, for his heart and home were always open to them."

The sun—the golden lamp of heaven—was trying desperately to reach through the dim laden air, and as I gazed across the campus at dear old Adams Hall and the stately Savage home, they seemed to say, "We have folded our comforting arms around students as they strolled the campus." Then with nods that seemed to lock secrets into their very foundations, they closed their eyes in remembrance. As my eyes misted with the ambient air, scenes passed in review through the corridors of memory, and easily could I have hugged every brick and wall.

CHAPTER 6

"Marriage is the earth's institution and is ordained by God.
Civilization and moral standards of a people can be judged by the
attitude they have toward marriage.
Nations or peoples who regard the wedding vows lightly have low
standards of morals. The higher the regard for marriage the
higher the standard of civilization."

—M. E. Dodd—

Union at Union

A BASEBALL ENTHUSIAST AND PLAYER, ELMON MONROE Dodd found that his sport was not exactly on the agenda for potential ministers, and his participation created objections by some of the brethren in ordaining this young man. But Monroe [as he became known] answered the questions of the council with such fervor and conviction that not one could shake their head or express any doubt. They knew God had called him, and during his sophomore year at Union, ordained him to the gospel ministry on Sunday, April 13, 1902, at the Trenton, Tennessee, Baptist Church.

Rev. A. P. Moore, with his attenuated frame, preached the ordination sermon. Deacon Senter, bank president and Sunday School superintendent, was secretary of the ordaining council. According to the *Herald Democrat* of Trenton, April 18, 1902:

> Last Sunday morning, Rev. M. E. Dodd, a prominent and worthy young man of this city, was ordained to the ministry of the Baptist church here. A presbytery consisting of Rev. Moore and Butler and the deacons of the Baptist church of this city met at the residence of J. M. Senter and examined the candidate. The presbytery approved and presented his claims to the church, which were endorsed by a unanimous vote of the members present. The ordination sermon was preached by Rev. A. P. Moore of this city in an instructive and forcible manner. J. M. Senter, in an appropriate way, delivered the charge to the church, and Rev. J. H. Butler presented the Bible with some timely admonitions.

A large audience was present and the services were interesting and impressive.

When they came by for the laying on of hands, the ministers felt very strongly the presence of a tower of strength, but none felt it as keenly as the young preacher being ordained, for the Master Himself laid His hands on his head that day.

Monroe was student pastor at several churches from 1902 to 1903 and took his first full-time pastorate in Fulton, Kentucky, January 1, 1904 — six months prior to graduating from college. At this time, he was also appointed as a missionary to Mexico by the Foreign Mission Board. While much was being accomplished in preparation for his life's work, there was also another factor that was in the offing. An excerpt from the *Shreveport Journal* throws some light on this situation, reporting that "at the time Monroe Dodd was attending Union University, he fell in love with the cake baker. She was none other than the president's daughter, Emma Savage." Emma provided more details. "Monroe had been coming to the house for quite awhile," she said, "to get a book or talk to Father, but I didn't think much about him until he came to live in our home along with other preacher boys. My father always tried to help them make their money go farther."

"I liked to make cakes," Emma said, "and one day, as I was baking, he came in and licked the spoon. It was a coconut cake; this was always his favorite. One thing I decided I was going to do was to break him from licking around the plate. I had made a devil's food this particular day, and was feeling a little devilish myself. So, I put pepper all around the plate. It wasn't long before he came in with the gleam in his eyes and fastened them on the cake. That was the last time he ever licked frosting from around the plate."

Autumn came as before, dressed in rich rare apparel; yet, this September 1903 would ever be delightfully different to an aggressive young ministerial senior and a lovely gentian-eyed miss who was very striking in appearance yet utterly feminine. Those velvet blue eyes of Emma's made Monroe's heart play a soft obligato.

The city of Jackson was blossomed out in street fair regalia. When Monroe went to get Emma for their first date, he took her to the carnival. They strolled along with the sky arching over them, bright with shimmerings from a golden moon. Love had been blooming in both their hearts for quite awhile, and this enchanted evening was doing everything within its power to add to the charm. In a fortune teller's booth, the soothsayer asked them in. He told the gypsy in all fairness that he did not believe in the power to foresee the future. The seerer smiled and reproached him for his mistrust of the mystic and then made a statement that almost converted young Dodd.

"You two are in love," she prophesied, "and are going to get married." There may be something to this, he gasped to himself, hardly daring to look at Emma. Not realizing, because of his condition, that any passerby could have come up with a similar statement. Any discerning eye could have made the same deduction. On their way back to the president's home, a silver moonbeam caught the highlights in Emma's hair, and Monroe noticed a little ringlet was out of place which was quite bewitching.

Their love continued and grew in beauty through the winter months as they watched Christmas come and go, followed closely by the new year 1904. That spring, Monroe graduated from Union University. Graduation gifts are something special, but a book entitled *Poems You Ought To Know* was unique and in a class by itself—Emma's gift. Inside she wrote, "With Best Wishes of Your Friend—E. Savage."

We flaunt words so easily now, that at times they seem to have no meaning at all. Friend is defined as "a person bound to another by affection, esteem, and intimacy." Emma's inscription, casual to us, had deep meaning for Monroe Dodd. It wasn't too long thereafter that Monroe said to Emma, "Completely, have I lost my heart to you."

The charming, cultured daughter of the president with her captivating personality and consecrated Christian character was exactly what Monroe wanted in a wife. He knew this was heavenly planning no words could express—yes, it was ineffable. Whether or not the dignified austere Dr. Savage had had this same heavenly vision about his own wife, Monroe didn't know, and the thought of approaching him and asking for his daughter's hand left him a little fearful.

Now ordinarily, the devil himself wouldn't have fazed him, but this was the daughter of the university president, whose stern countenance Monroe did not care to face. His modest fifty-dollar-a-month salary did not dampen his ardor; yet, he knew he must do the honorable and noble thing. While at his church in Fulton, he learned that his intended father-in-law was to be in Mississippi, so he wrote him a letter announcing his desire to marry Emily, the name Dr. Savage exclusively used for his daughter.

Waiting for a reply was most taxing on the young pastor's nerves. It finally came bearing the message "You have my consent and blessing; my feeling for you is already that of a son."

It was the desire of Monroe and Emma that her father conduct the ceremony. But Dr. Savage insisted that the sacred service should be performed by the pastor of the bride's church. Their pastor was Rev. G. S. Williams of the First Baptist Church of Jackson. It was his duty, Papa Savage contended, and it surpassed even the right of the father to conduct the rites. Though disappointed, they bowed to his judgment. So admirable did Monroe consider the elder Savage's ethics, that he adopted them for his own. Dr. Dodd never performed a wedding ceremony for one belonging to another church without the sanction and consent of the pastor of the bride's church. Dr. Dodd, in his ministry, often spoke about the sanctity of marriage. "Marriage is the earth's institution and is ordained by God. Civilization and moral standards of a people can be judged by the attitude they have toward marriage. Nations or peoples who regard the wedding vows lightly have low standards of morals. The higher the regard for marriage the higher the standard of civilization."

Tennessee in October can be alluringly lovely, and the weather was definitely in collusion with the nuptial. The wedding took place in the Savage residence at 604 E. College Street, October 10, 1904. Just being married on this day was excitement enough, but no, Emma was also appointed by the Board the same day as a foreign missionary.

At eight o'clock in the evening, to the strains of wedding music, the bride and groom came down the stairway into the parlor. Emma's blue eyes were set off by a delicate tan silk gown rich with golden tones from shades of October. Monroe's slick-bottomed shoes were giving him trouble, and as he caught a sidelong glance at the foot of the stairway where his Alpha Tau Omega fraternity brothers were gathered, his knees began to shake and with the help of the new shoes, he almost stumbled down the stairway.

Amid the flurry of rice, Monroe and Emma left the stately president's home that was the scene of so many mixed emotions and heartaches that come with the struggle for higher education—struggles that speak in tones so low that they are beyond the ken of everyone except those who pursue under similar conditions.

College days were over, and this was a happy time as Monroe led his bride to the station and boarded the train. As they left, Emma's father didn't say goodbye. He just said, "Emily, I'm going to miss you next Wednesday night." She had always accompanied him to church. The whistle blew, and the wheels of the iron king thundered away. Dr. Savage stood by the track; he could feel a moisture in his eyes. His was a solitary cry on the inside that only the father of a daughter would understand. Goodbye, Emily—goodbye.

Two newspapers contained nice articles about the marriage. Then the couple went on to Fulton where the young pastor's congregation awaited them. The little flock had raised $150 for a wedding gift which Monroe and Emma used to furnish their small four-room cottage. "We didn't even have pillows," Emma said. Monroe used part of the money for books. His first library consisted of the Bible, *Preacher's Homiletic Commentary*, and the *Life of George Washington*.

In addition to the $150 gift, the members of the church raised their pastor's salary $10, which Dr. Dodd used facetiously years later when he would remark, "That makes Mrs. Dodd worth ten dollars a month to me."

It was not without hesitation that Dr. Dodd accepted the Fulton pastorate, for he had received what he thought to be a divine impression to become a missionary. Seeking to follow God's divine leadership, he offered himself to the Foreign Mission Board for service in Persia where the Board was considering opening a mission. The Board, however, decided otherwise and appointed Dr. Dodd as a missionary to Mexico. The appointment came after he had accepted the Fulton pastorate and had been on the field for some months. After much prayer and consideration, he followed what he thought to be divine leadings, resigned the Fulton church, and accepted the appointment.

Four months after their October wedding, they found themselves in Mexico ready for whatever the Lord would have them do. There is not enough space here to give in detail the events of the trip to their field of labor; but, it is sufficient to report that after three railroad wrecks, they arrived at the mission post. For four months, everything seemed to go wrong, God seemed to be leading in other directions. Meanwhile, the Fulton church kept urging them to return and accept again the work there. After three months of prayer, Dr. and Mrs. Dodd were led into the clear light and came to a definite conviction that God's will had not been fully wrought in their going to Mexico. Arriving at this conclusion after many infallible proofs had been given, they decided that the Lord would have them return to Fulton. So after a four-month absence, he took up the work in Fulton once again.

Baker James Cauthen was Executive Secretary of the Foreign Mission Board when I called in the late fifties for any information on the Dodds. They sent me copies of pages from the *Foreign Mission Journal* and the book *Thirty Years in Mexico*. Pictures and descriptions of their illustrious backgrounds met my eyes. "Why?" I thought. Then I heard: "My ways are not your ways." And some of those ways we will never see this side of the gates of glory. However, the magnitude of this mission experience was the beginning of a new fervor in the hearts of Dr. and Mrs. Dodd that kindled the fire to the ends of the earth. It raised the curtain and gave birth to a missionary zeal they had never felt before. This was God's way.

CHAPTER 7

Iron Lace

IN 1912, THE DODDS SAID BONJOUR TO LOUISIANA, embarking on a journey that would ultimately have impact around the world. Coming to Shreveport in 1912—they left their footprints behind at First Baptist of Fulton, Kentucky; First Baptist of Paducah, Kentucky; and Twenty-second and Walnut Streets Baptist in Louisville, Kentucky. Shreveport was a north Louisiana town which had a population of 28,000, and the First Baptist Church had a membership of 582. Pretty good numbers for 1912 in a state that was looked upon as a mission field needing help for its people.

Mrs. Dodd, in an interview, was asked, "Why did you come?"

"He saw an opportunity," she answered. Yes, Dr. Dodd saw Louisiana laid out before him; but not until God's call turned him in that direction. "Behold!—Before thee an open door. The doors are wide open in Louisiana. Listen! I have work for you to do. Hear my words and do them."

THE TITANIC

M. E. Dodd's maiden voyage to Shreveport collided with the sinking of the Titanic. His first church service was April 7, 1912, and the following Sunday, April 14, the Titanic started sinking and was completely submerged by the next morning. His ministry was incipient, but with the sinking of the unsinkable Titanic, mockingly laughed about in circles that said, "Even God couldn't sink it," you could hear him preaching . . .

Christ is the captain of this ship—it is unsinkable and there are enough lifeboats for each of you!! No first, second, or third class—no matter which

deck you are on, there is only one deck at the foot of the cross. All who put
their hand in the hand of the captain shall be saved; come forward and
accept Christ. There is room in the lifeboat for you!

Even though modern technology was beginning to be apparent in
American life, your feet could still feel the dirt roads, and the horse-and-
buggy users did not appreciate the new motor-driven vehicles coming into
their territory. Upon his arrival in Shreveport, Dr. Dodd (like the new auto-
mobiles) immediately demonstrated his aggressiveness. He had a passion for
making pastoral calls, and in one year walked over a thousand miles and rode
street cars to make fifteen hundred calls. Impressed by his annual report to
the church, members of his congregation gave him an automobile — they did
not call it a car; it was an automobile! He became the first Shreveport pastor
to use such a conveyance in his work. It was called a horseless carriage — the
king of travel — and he was using it for the King of Kings. With this stream-
lined beauty, his pastoral calls doubled, and he filled many more outside
speaking engagements in special services. Thus, his ministry broadened and
multiplied by the application of modern mechanics.

With all the advantages that the new automobile provided, it did not
prevent one mild dilemma in the Dodd household. The manufacturers
provided only one bumper, and the debate was whether it should go on the
back or the front. Dr. Dodd urged that it go on the rear; but, his good wife,
knowing that her husband was prone to go forward more than backwards,
reasoned that it should be on the front. The matter ended as most such inci-
dents between man and wife do, in a compromise. Of course, the bumper
went in front!

THE FLYING PARSON

It wasn't long after this that Dr. Dodd realized his automobile didn't fly,
and he needed something more breathtaking and swift; so, he started using
the airplane. One newspaper highlight said he was the first person in
Shreveport and probably the nation to use this cloud chariot to reach
speaking engagements. Among his first flights was to Chickasha, Oklahoma,
where he was to deliver the baccalaureate address at the State Teachers
College. He flew in an early-model open-cockpit one-passenger plane, and
his pilot was Lieutenant Sam Alexander. The pilot used a road map to find
his way to the Canadian River whose course he then followed to Chickasha.

Learning of Dr. Dodd's plan to come by plane, the Chamber of
Commerce arranged a big reception at the landing field. However, the pilot

did not know where the field was. Instead, he flew over Chickasha and Dr. Dodd, recognizing the college campus, pointed to it. The noise of the plane, the pulse of the open air, and cotton-stuffed ears rendered conversation impossible. Mistaking this gesture as instructions to land, the pilot made a landing right on the campus. He taxied to a stop a few feet from the auditorium where Dr. Dodd was to speak. Meanwhile, the reception party was left stranded at the airfield several miles away.

Going by plane required only one day to make this appointment; whereas, by other means of transportation, three days would have been consumed, and Dr. Dodd had a passion for conserving time. He considered time "the stuff of which life is made" and therefore, not to be squandered. This was the beginning of his slipping into the sky and gliding away. He felt "heaven high," and he soon became known all over the country as the "Flying Parson" which newspapers everywhere picked up with photographs and stories.

THE YANKS ARE COMING!

August 1914 arrived, and our countrymen were overcome with bewilderment and painful surprise by the outbreak of war in Europe. President Wilson immediately announced neutrality and that "we must be impartial in thought as well as action." America could not sit in judgement. If Europe chose to fight, that was her affair, but we would not get involved. But when April 1917 rolled around, the American people knew war could no longer be avoided.

There had been attacks by German submarines on our commerce. Everyone stood behind Wilson's grief-toned declaration that "the right is more precious than peace and that the United States must perforce go to war, not for any selfish end, but in defense of the principles for which it stood."

Yes, as the song said, "We're coming over, we're coming over, and we won't be back 'til it's over over there!"

Our boys were marching, marching. Only God (there are no atheists in foxholes), thoughts of their families, girlfriends, and music got our wearied mud-covered, cootie infested doughboys through this diabolical and fiendish war. (Our infantrymen in the United States Army got the name doughboy during the Mexican War because they used dough to make their hot meals. After fighting, there would be flour on their uniforms—thus the enemy nicknamed them.)

Most of the songs were romantic, tender, and very emotional. "The Long, Long Trail" spoke of winding to the land of dreams. It's a "Long Way to

Dr. Dodd as a chaplain during World War I. He volunteered in 1914 and went overseas in 1918 to serve with the Second Army in France.

Tipperary" pointed out that above everything else, that doughboy wanted to get back to the girl he adored. It became one of the best known songs of the war mainly because these fighting men made a marching tune out of this love ballad. Singing as they marched kept them going!

Dr. Dodd volunteered for the chaplaincy in 1914 while pastoring in Shreveport, but accepted an assignment of duty with the Young Men's Christian Association. In this service, he was to become spiritual counselor and minister to thousands of men at home and abroad. For several months, he was stationed at Camp Beauregard, Louisiana, and then he made speaking tours of various cantonments.

In September 1918, he sailed overseas and was attached to the Second Army under General Bullard. The Germans and Allies were gripped in the final death struggle of World War I when Dr. Dodd was to experience one of the most dangerous and thrilling missions of his life.

He was at Sezerais, France, when a request came for him to go to Mont Mouzon on the opposite side of the Mozelle River and minister to soldiers at an advance post on the mountain. This contingent had been without service for weeks and were also without benefit of any minister. The only means of transportation to the isolated group of soldiers who were dug into the side of the mountain was by motorcycle with a baby bathtub attachment. A red-headed sergeant from Indiana was the driver. Dr. Dodd clambered into the little sidecar and set out over a rough and winding mountain road for the front lines. They passed through villages laid low by gunfire; all you could see was ruin and rubble. In the distance, the roar of artillery could be heard. They were nearing the front. Sentries along the route halted the red-headed motorcyclist and demanded identification. The messenger responded by showing his credentials and urging the importance of his mission. Orders must get through to the front line. Finally, they reached the last sentry post and just ahead, the bursts of shells sounded like thunder. The Germans were laying down a heavy barrage in an attempt to break the communication lines. Then came a moment of great decision for Dr. Dodd. Should he take the risk of going through that barrage? As Dr. Dodd pondered over his fears and excuses, the sergeant spoke up:

"Sir, you don't have to go any farther. You had better stay here."

Dr. Dodd meditated a moment. He offered a silent prayer.

What would the men up at the front think of him? What would the soldiers he had ministered to think of him? What would Jesus do?

Up ahead, men were fighting, bleeding, dying, without a minister to comfort them to bury their dead—what would they say? Yes, he must go forward!

"Let's be going," Dr. Dodd said, as he fastened his gas mask and tightened up his helmet straps and took a firmer hold on to the side of his little compartment. "Red" the driver stepped on the gas, and the motorcycle sped forward. At the edge of a clearing, the motorcyclist slowed down and observed the barrage. The shells were falling a few hundred yards ahead on the highway.

Then Red spoke, "You notice those shells are falling at intervals of thirty seconds. We'll ease up as close as we can and right after a shell falls, run ahead so we can get through under the next one."

Cautiously they approached the area where the shells were bursting and annihilating everything in sight. The engines of destruction were in full swing.

After an explosion, the motorcycle shot forward over the shell-torn highway at break-neck speed and had barely cleared the area when the next shell came overhead and burst perilously close behind.

At the end of the harrowing journey, Red turned to Dr. Dodd and said, "Padre, are you a praying man?" Dr. Dodd explained that he was.

"I just knew you could really pray," said Red. "I've come to this mountain fourteen times, and this is the first time I ever got through without trouble—didn't even have a blowout."

"Yes," Dr. Dodd said, "the powerful arm of God has been around us giving His protection."

Shreveport, his pastorate, his home, and family on Fairfield Avenue would have to wait awhile. He was overseas six months—for which the church had graciously given him leave to serve his country. When he returned from France after World War I, his awareness that family prayer and faith in God is what has made America great and strong was more discerning than ever.

"Let's never forget it," he said, as his baby girl threw her arms around his neck and sighed, "God bless Daddy."

Yes, it was over—over there—but really beginning over here. He had felt the strength of God's arm, and now he was back in the land of "Iron Lace."

Whenever people were asked to write about Louisiana, it was always titled "Lovely Louisiana." Dr. Dodd's mind moved in the same tone and waxed rather poetic in his writings; referring to Louisiana as a fair maiden:

This lovely lady is the proud possessor of the richest riches of all the earth. They are the riches of romance and religion; the riches of adventurous pioneering; the riches of golden sunsets; the riches of golden dreams of orange blossoms and silver streams; the riches of vast forests and fertile fields; the riches of snowy cotton plantations of rice and fishes; the riches of liquid gold from the overflowing and ever flowing oil wells.

Yes! Louisiana was *bel voir*—beautiful to see in all of its magnolia splendor. She is sometimes called the "Sweet State" because of the fields of sugar cane. However, along with this sweetness, we cannot forget the bayou—torrid, busy, moss-hung cypress trees growing in the Louisiana swampianus—a sight to behold at sunset. Yet within this beauty to the eye, there are satanic forces in the form of alligators, water moccasins, and many pestilential creatures. Dr. Dodd knew there was a pestilence in the state—deadly and morally harmful. He saw the beauty, but he saw the people—music to his eyes. They needed the Lord Jesus Christ.

The lacy ironwork balconies in the French Quarter of New Orleans is a trademark. It is ornamental and historical. The "Iron Lace" between the joints of wood in beautiful homes gives strength as well as beauty—strength like the alligator and the beauty of the moss hanging from the trees.

While striking the same chord, Dr. Dodd knew how to blend the iron and the lace. The most common and useful metal, iron has great hardness, strength, firmness, and is unyielding. An "iron" will belonged to Dr. Dodd tempered with "lace." God combined the two in him, and when Southern Baptists needed iron and lace, they called on M. E. Dodd.

We say, "Au revoir" to feathered foliage illuminating the countryside— a tapestry of rich color—nature's canvas displaying "Before thee, an open door."

"HEIL HITLER"

Adolf Hitler spread death as no man has ever done before. He hated Christianity and said it was a religion for weaklings; he blamed the Jews for all the evils of the world.

Before me, on my desk, was a published copy of an address delivered by M. E. Dodd before the Baptist World Congress in Berlin, Germany, 1934, entitled "The Gospel for Today."

My thoughts immediately went to the cancer of hatred Hitler had in his heart for Christians. How could this crowd of Baptists from all over the world be in Berlin in any safety—especially Dr. Dodd—with the words that would issue forth from this great orator?

History came to life! Through the years, Hitler had been moving steadily toward dictatorship. The aging president, Paul Von Hindenburg, named Hitler as Chancellor of Germany in 1933, and anyone who opposed him would be killed.

Hindenburg died in August of 1934, and Hitler ruled Germany completely. With all of this in mind, I felt a gentle urging from the Lord to look on the flyleaf of Dr. Dodd's manuscript. "I have looked at it," I said to myself. "I know everything that is there."

"Look again!"

As I looked, chills ran up my spine. It wasn't only 1934, but August when this message was delivered—the exact same year and month that Hitler became dictator. Hitler's power was gigantic, godlike, grasping, and generative. He *was* Germany!

My fears were confirmed by reflectings contained in Dr. Dodd's book, *Girdling the Globe for God*.

In Berlin in 1934, Dr. Dodd, president of the Southern Baptist Convention, posed with George Truett (right) president of the Baptist World Alliance. At this conference, in Hitler's shadow, Dodd delivered his sermon entitled "The Gospel for Today."

It had not been easy for these representative Christians to come to Berlin. Many obstacles had intervened. The Congress had been invited in 1918 but the World War prevented. Then it should have met there in 1923 but the devastating work of the World War upon Germany made it impossible for them to care for it at that time.

Finally, when the World Alliance accepted the invitation to meet in Berlin in 1933, the worldwide depression interposed and the Executive Committee postponed it for a year. Then when it was voted to meet in Berlin in 1934, a vicious anti-German propaganda interposed and sought to prevent the Baptists from coming to Berlin at this time, creating fears as to what would occur.

We had been told that if we should meet in Berlin, we would face the dilemma either of keeping our mouths shut on our great fundamental principles and thereby be classed as cowards, or else of speaking our mind on vital questions and subjecting ourselves to arrest at the hands of the Nazis. Much of this turned out to be propaganda and there was a real welcome from the German government and the German people.

Not only was the Congress accorded the utmost liberty of expression, but its messages were given wide hearing in the newspaper and over the radio. This was a great surprise because one prominent Congress leader said, "We may be free to say what we wish, but it will be within the walls of the meeting place and will never get outside." His mind is now entirely disabused.

From stories, feature articles and photographs of the Congress which appeared daily in Berlin papers and throughout Germany, German people everywhere were asking, "Who are these Baptists?" Some thought it was a new political party.

During this crucial period in world history, Dr. George W. Truett was president of the Baptist World Alliance, and Dr. M. E. Dodd was president of the Southern Baptist Convention. No doubt, the iron arm of God was over us again; but, a seed was planted that could only have come at this time—before World War II began in 1939. It did not mean Hitler was not lurking in the shadows. Deceptively, diabolically, and viciously, he was waiting for the right time.

Many could ask, "Why keep trying to go to Berlin?" The Bible tells us to go into all the world—and Baptists, after much prayer, have always gone where they were needed—on the paths that God wanted them to trod.

Listen to the sweeping ocean of music from Kaiserdam Hall in Berlin where ten thousand people representing every race stood to sing, each in his own language, the National Anthem of the Kingdom of God, "All Hail the Power of Jesus Name." They spoke a babble of forty tongues, yet their spirit and purpose were one.

Dr. Dodd's address to the Baptist congress was awe inspiring, as the excerpts indicate:

Let us come to the New Testament. I believe we can find the remedy for the world's woes in the gospel according to Hebrews. There is recognition of the need for a varied presentation of God's way according to the time and place of the people. In the former times God spoke through the voice of prophets. In later ages He spoke by His written Word. In these last days He has spoken in His Son. . . .

. . . God's remedy is always adapted to the condition of the patient at the time the application is to be made. And yet it is the same remedy always. Water takes the form of the vessel in which it is placed. But it is the water and not the vessel that slakes thirst and saves life. . . .

. . . Hebrews climaxes with the grand statement, "Jesus Christ, the same yesterday, and today, and forever." And He is that water of life. This is the one universal drink. People may have their national drinks—Russian vodka, Mexican pulche, German beer, Scotch gin, English ale, French wine, American liquor—but water is common to all, sufficient for all, best for all. . . .

. . . This same Jesus is also the light of the world which points the way for men to walk. Light at different periods or places may come from a tallow candle, an oil lamp or an incandescent electric bulb, but all of these gather their light from one source, which is the sun. Whatever the light be by which men walk in a given period, He Who is the Light of the world is the source of all their light, and He lighteth every man that cometh into the world. . . .

. . . Man without this faith, without this God, is a ship without a rudder, a star without a course, a vagrant comet, orphaned in the universe, a weltering chaos of despair, lost, lost, lost! . . .

. . . Brotherhood means that Christians of whatever name or of whatever faith or of whatever rank or of whatever color in all parts of the world are one in Christ. . . .

. . . God hath made of one blood all men, and that blood is the blood of Christ. The ground is level at Calvary. One is your Master, even Christ, and all ye are brethren. In Christ there can be no castes or classes or ranks. . . .

. . . Ye are all a royal priesthood, princes of the blood, and "noblesse oblige" is yours. In Christ there is no place for racial prejudice, bitterness, or hatred. We be brethren. . . .

. . . The world needs a tie that binds, and that tie has been forged in the blood of Jesus Christ on the cross. This universal brotherhood, which comes from contact with Christ on the cross, creates character, confidence, conviction, consecration, power, and majesty. All other brotherhoods are shallow, surface, superficial affairs. . . .

. . . We belong to Heaven first, then to others, . . . Our citizenship in the kingdom of God should be stronger and should bind us closer together than any other relationship on earth. . . .

. . . This gospel for today has the greatest opportunity of all time and should have the most vigorous application by those who believe it. We who profess it should really believe it—believe it deeply, believe it passionately. The zeal of God's House has not eaten up very many of us as it did our Master. The zeal and passion and self-sacrifice with which the founders and promoters of Communism have lived and labored are not only a challenge to us, but they condemn our lackadaisical, half-hearted, half-believing, half-doubting ways. One was asked why infidels are so successful and the paradoxical answer was because they believe so profoundly. . . .

. . . We stand upon the threshold of the most challenging hour that Christianity has ever known. Christianity is not a fair-weather religion, never has been, never can be. It started on a cross; it moved forward through a grave. The blood of martyrs has always been the seed of the church, and it is still true that without the shedding of blood there is no remission. Times like these have always given the prophets of God their greatest chance. . . .

. . . Would to God we might capture, and be captured by, the adventurous and pioneering spirit of the first century Christians. That spirit sent them across the Roman Empire with torches to light the world to a new day. . . .

. . . Daring to live the poetry we sing, to live the gospel we preach, we may win the world for our Christ and His God. As a Japanese poet said 300 years ago. "If you would be a poet, your life must be a poem." So we say now, if you would be a Christian, your life must be a sermon.

The swastika is an ancient symbol used as an ornament or a religious sign in the form of a cross with arms bent. It was later adopted as a symbol for Germany and became one of the most hated symbols in the history of man. It came to stand for all the evil associated with the Nazis as they gained control of Europe before and during World War II. After the allies defeated Germany in 1945, they banned the display of the swastika emblem.

After requesting an interview with Gandhi, Dr. Dodd received a postcard from the Indian independence leader asking him to visit. Dr. and Mrs. Dodd visited with Mahatma Gandhi in India during their "Girdling the Globe for God" mission tour in 1934.

Hitler's life has fled—and streams of life circulate not, and yet, the Third Reich and Führer are alive and well. People still march to celebrate Nazism, which has come to our beloved land. Our young people are holding high the swastika and worshipping Adolf Hitler. They even bear his birthdate on their notebooks and backpacks in our schools. We must hear their longings and lead them to the edge of the infinite in Jesus.

During the war, our service men called the swastika a twisted cross. Hitler twisted it in the palm of his hand. We must untwist it with the nail-scarred hand.

"YOU ARE MY SUNSHINE"

Mahatma Gandhi

Mahatma Gandhi said, "Be the change you're trying to create."

Dr. Dodd's interview with Gandhi came about in a unique way—in a class by itself. Having no personal contacts in India close to Gandhi, he decided to write to him directly requesting an interview. Following this bold

Louisiana governor and songwriter James "Jimmy" Davis was a member of Dodd's congregation. Here, Davis (left) is sworn in as governor by W. D. Sandifer (at microphone). M. E. Dodd is seated on the far right.

method, he found in his mail upon arrival in Berlin a handwritten penny postal card from India. It bore the salutation, "Dear Friend," and he could not make out the signature at first. He almost tossed the card aside when he strained once more to decipher the writer's name. This time he made out the letter "M," then a "K," and then like a flash, the letters "G A N D H I M. K." Gandhi! The message read: "Dear Friend, I shall be happy to receive both Mrs. Dodd and yourself when you reach India."

In a *Time* magazine article written in 1928 about Gandhi, the "Soul Thrust" was mentioned. Indians spoke not of howitzers nor of horsepower, but rather of how to evoke from teeming millions a cumulative "soul thrust" which would rock the world. One and all, they deferred to the Mahatma: "The Great Soul." This man held more people in his hands than any other person. He was bursting with mob-igniting spirit.

"Gandhi is not a Christian," Dr. Dodd once said. "He has many Christian ideas. He has Christian ideals for a just social order. He has studied all religions. He has read the New Testament. He believes that Jesus was one of the world's great religious teachers, but not the Son of God, in any sense different from others."

The interview with Gandhi was enlightening and Dr. Dodd left him a greater admirer than when he went. He only wished that this great man were a Christian. What a power that would have been!

Governor Jimmie Davis

I wanted to title this section "You Are My Sunshine" to show Dr. Dodd's thoughts on political leaders and politics, so I wrote Governor Davis to secure his permission for its inclusion here. The letter I received from his staff read, "Governor Davis is currently in the hospital. He is 100 years on the calendar, but would be honored to have the title in the book."

Dr. M. E. Dodd believed that a preacher who used his pulpit for partisan political purposes desecrated the altar of God. But the minister who avoided taking a stand in political affairs when there was a clear-cut moral issue failed in his duty to his church, to society, and to God. Many who do not understand this distinction are prone to abuse pastors who at times make themselves heard and felt in political campaigns. These critics fail to grasp the difference between partisan politics and moral issues.

It was Dr. Dodd's custom to preach a sermon on Christian citizenship prior to general elections. All new voters were invited as special guests, and he emphasized to them their responsibilities as citizens.

Jimmie Davis had been a member of Dr. Dodd's church for many years and was teaching at Dodd College when he was elected to several public offices. In 1938 Davis's campaign for city commissioner marked one of the occasions on which Dr. Dodd took an active part, for there was a moral issue involved.

Gambling was rampant in the city at the time, and the incumbent was lax in his duty to suppress it. He was also being supported by gambling and vice elements. The leading gambler of the city was a strong supporter of Davis's opponent, and with loud drumming in front and no soldiers behind, he boasted that when his man won he would run Dr. Dodd out of town. Instead, his man lost and was sent to a chain gang.

When Davis ran for governor the first time, Dr. Dodd felt impelled to open action.

The opponents of Davis for governor engaged in a scurrilous attack upon his character as a man. These attacks were published in the newspapers and in campaign literature. I knew they were untrue and that Davis was a man of high character. I felt it my duty to speak out. I will always defend any member of my congregation whenever I see his character and reputation attacked. I knew that if Jimmie were elected he would move to Baton Rouge and transfer his membership to the Baptist church there, so I wrote the pastor, Dr. J. Norris Palmer. In the letter, I extolled Jimmie's virtues and charged as false these attacks on his character. I also gave a copy of this letter to the Davis Campaign Headquarters with full liberty to use it as they saw fit.

They sent a copy of it to every Evangelical preacher in the state for delivery on the Saturday preceding the election on the following Tuesday. I do not know what effect that letter had on the outcome of the election.

Observers, however, will tell you that it was a valuable asset to the election of Davis as governor.

There were other turbulent excursions into political fields. Sometimes, Dr. Dodd would go to Washington with other leaders — talk with presidents, the Senate, and Congress to help keep our nation Christian. Dr. Dodd had sound judgement, farsightedness, and skill in dealing with public problems. The Iron Lace was always present.

We are guilty of not giving leaders full credit when they act or sing, but Jimmie Davis had political wisdom and was a statesman skilled in public and government affairs. However, we shall close this door on a light note. "You Are My Sunshine" became his calling card. It crossed the Atlantic to England, where King George VI declared it his favorite song. It was translated into over thirty languages including Russian and Japanese. We do not always remember the great political accomplishments, but rather things that touch the heart. Davis passed away in 2000 at the age of 101 years — Sunshine evermore!

Huey P. Long

The "sunshine" in the political arena continued with the "Kingfish" Huey Long, nicknamed for his promise to make "Every Man a King." That was his slogan. He was called a dictator, and many feared he would become president, but he was shot in 1935 at the Louisiana state capitol in Baton Rouge and died two days later. However, before he became governor of Louisiana and a United States senator, an unusual incident occurred which brought the colorful Huey P. Long into the membership of Dr. Dodd's church.

Long was a Baptist for several years before coming to Shreveport upon being elected Public Service Commissioner in 1918. The first efforts to get Long to transfer his church letter from Winnfield to Shreveport failed after the usual approach and procedure had been used. Huey knew that he had many political enemies in the First Baptist Church, including his principal foe, the mayor of Shreveport.

The time came, however, when the annual report of the church was made. It was an excellent report showing many new members and a good financial condition. The day that the report was published in the Shreveport newspapers, Dr. Dodd met Huey on the street. They engaged in a conversation, and a small crowd gathered around them.

"Hey, Doc," Huey began, "I see where you had a mighty fine year at your church, but how did you do it with all of those scalawags like that old mayor in your congregation?"

"Well, Huey," Dr. Dodd replied, "we always have room for one more. How about you being the next one to join?"

The little group laughed, and so did Huey. He liked Dr. Dodd's reply, and on the following Sunday, he attended services, tendered his letter, and as he remarked, "added another scalawag to the membership."

Franklin D. Roosevelt

In 1995, the *Austin American Statesman* headlined an article on F. D. R.— "Love him or hate him, Roosevelt changed America in ways that are still felt every day."

In the 1933 *Shreveport Journal*, an article entitled "Dodd heads Delegation to call on President Roosevelt" reported that a delegation of Southern Baptists arranged to visit the White House and present a letter to President Roosevelt commending him for his anti-war message to foreign rulers. At the same time, they deplored the return of beer and protested a repeal of the Eighteenth Amendment. Dr. Dodd was appointed to head the delegation which included one representative from each of the eighteen participating states.

The Louisiana *Baptist Message* of 1934 continued with stories regarding the Baptists' stand on consumption of alcohol. Dr. Dodd was vocal on the issue in an article entitled "Saloons Open—Schools Close."

In a recent address, Dr. M. E. Dodd, president of the Southern Baptist Convention made a most significant statement concerning a paradoxical condition that came about during the latter part of the year. He said, "The year 1933 will go down in history as the year the saloons (or the legalized liquor traffic) were opened and the schools were closed. In the years to come, when things can be seen in true lights; when passions that stirred men's souls at this time have been forgotten, historians will have their opportunity to tell the true and unbiased story of 1933. Would you not like to look far enough into the future to read what they shall write about America's backward step in bringing back the worst enemy humanity has ever known—that strange psychological twist that caused people to think of demon alcohol as a panacea for all our nation's ills?

Historians unquestionably will dwell upon the gullibility of the American people in 1933 as attaining a climax in puerile imbecility. The people believed a lot of lies the liquor interests put out about liquor bringing back prosperity which the liquor people themselves did not believe.

Well, we have the saloons and liquor back in all its satanic glory! But where is the prosperity it promised to bring with it? Here is what has come with the legalized liquor trade. In Shreveport, arrests for drunkenness took a jump to the tune of 300 percent increase; arrests for drunk driving has stepped forward 300 percent also. We do not have the figures on the increase of fatal accidents from drunk driving, but we know it has just about kept pace with the baleful advance. Liquor people are urging certain officials to not make these figures public, for they say, the figures are detrimental to their bloody business. So much for the 'triumphant success' of the saloons.

Now, what of the public schools, the greatest institutions in the country, excepting only the churches? Statistics tell us that during the latter part of 1933 when people were celebrating the opening of the saloons, 2,000 schools were closed for lack of funds; 5,000 more schools have been compelled to shorten their sessions; 1,000,000 pupils have been thrown out of school and 200,000 school teachers, who have spent years preparing for their worthy vocation, have been thrown out of work.

Well, we have the saloons—why worry?

In Dr. Dodd's address, nearly seventy years ago, he also asked, "What will we say in the future?" This is the future—what do we say?

In First Baptist Church, Shreveport's newspaper, *The Church Chimes*, 1949, Dr. Dodd wrote in the pastor's paragraph:

A good woman asked me what she could say to her neighbors who persisted with invitations for her to drink with them. They are lovely people, but they drink regularly. They simply could not understand why she would not drink with them. What harm was there in it? It did not hurt them, how could it hurt her? She wanted me to give her the answer. I said, "Tell them you do not drink because alcohol is a narcotic poison and a habit-forming drug which requires more and more to satisfy the drinker. Furthermore, you have two children and a husband; your neighbor has one child and a husband, which makes seven people. Out of every seven who drink, one will become an alcoholic. Ask your neighbor if she is willing for her child or husband to become an alcoholic or if she would like to see one of your family an alcoholic?" There is only one thing to do with intoxicating liquor, and that is to avoid it as you would a poisonous snake, which it is in reality.

Many fine denominations have fought the good fight. Someone said, "You Baptists are against drinking, aren't you?"

Yes, but it's deeper than that. First Corinthians 8:13 teaches that if I do something—even if I can—and it makes my brother stumble, I will not do it.

Are we our brother's keeper?

Dr. Dodd understood the swinging pendulum of time. Washington, D.C., and President Franklin Roosevelt were on his agenda many times. There were many turbulent excursions into political fields. Dr. Dodd could feel the shifting of political winds, and God gave him guided, gifted, brilliant words. He was there not just for Baptists, but for all Christians and citizens of our great country.

There was not agreement in all of Roosevelt's proclamations, but Dr. Dodd praised his leadership. Dr. Dodd considered F. D. R. one of the greatest political personalities he had ever known. Roosevelt had a convincing and winsome personality that was disarming.

Dr. Dodd offered the prayer at more than one session of the House of Representatives and once in the Senate. The latter occasion afforded him an opportunity to meet Harry S. Truman, who was then vice-president. They met first in the Senate cloakroom.

"I'm glad to have a Baptist come pray for us," the genial Truman said to Dr. Dodd, "because I'm a Baptist myself."

Truman led Dr. Dodd to the Senate Chamber and had him stand on the upper platform beside him instead of the one usually used by speakers who are not members of the Senate. At the time, the war was drawing to a close. It was April 1945, so Dr. Dodd prayed that the Senate might be given wisdom to act upon the eventual peace treaty and made a special supplication for the vice-president. As he closed his prayer and turned to leave the platform, Vice-President Truman looked into Dr. Dodd's face, shook his hand, and with tears in his eyes said, "Thank you. I want you to pray for us often, and come again." That day, Dr. Dodd dined in the Senate dining room with Senators Overton and Ellender and Congressmen Brooks and Allen. Overton said of Truman at this luncheon, "His thinking is crystal clear; his honesty and integrity are without question. He is loyal to his friends, and he is gifted at picking capable helpers."

Perhaps at the time they were thinking about the probability of Truman becoming president, for it was known that Roosevelt was in failing health. Two weeks later, Roosevelt died, and Harry Truman became president of the United States.

Of all political figures, great and small, Dr. Dodd ranked Charles Evans Hughes, former Chief Justice of the United States Supreme Court, as the "most majestic mentality I have ever met."

My heartfelt gratitude goes out to Dr. Dodd, our Baptist leaders and forefathers, who put their feet in paths untrod and made it easier for us to walk with heads held high and carry the torch full blaze.

Later, as I stood on the boardwalk overlooking Galveston Bay and watched the waves beat against the sea wall with prodigious strength, I thought of the storms of life and how we survive them. Then the thunder roared and said, "Survival only by faith."

NEW ORLEANS SEMINARY

At the Southern Baptist Convention in 1915, Dr. Dodd met in a hotel room with seven other Baptist leaders in the initial movement that resulted in another great denominational enterprise. The topic of the meeting was the establishment of a Baptist Theological Seminary in New Orleans.

Among those present were Dr. John T. Christian, Dr. George H. Crutcher, Dr. P. I. Lipsey, Dr. Dodd, and a few others. The men drew up a memorial which they requested Dr. Dodd to present to the Southern Baptist Convention at the Asheville, North Carolina, session the following year. He was named chairman of the committee on plans, conducted a vast amount of correspondence, and did a lot of work in preparing the plea to the convention. In 1917, the convention met in New Orleans and Dr. Dodd presented the report, which was like a wind-surging tide in the treetops.

His words were followed by action endorsing the proposal. When the convention met at Hot Springs, Arkansas, in 1918, Dr. Dodd's military duties kept him from attending. At this convention, the matter of financing the establishment of a seminary in New Orleans was a vexing problem. In the midst of the sessions, a telegram was received from Dr. Dodd, announcing a pledge of $25,000 from the First Baptist Church of Shreveport to the school. This was considerable currency in this year of our Lord. You could feel the convention knew they were on spiritual territory, and the wind now was like a breath of heaven.

Dr. B. H. Dement, who had been chosen to head the new institution, declared that this pledge was the incident which inspired the convention to make the necessary appropriation for the establishment of the Baptist Bible Institute (the name at that time).

Today the New Orleans Baptist Theological Seminary stands as a citadel for those who give their lives to the Lord's work. Here our leaders study for their high calling. It is a fine tribute to a labor of love that one of the buildings of the institution bore this inscription: "M. E. Dodd Administration Building." At this time, two buildings—faculty offices and a dorm—are named for Dr. Dodd.

A HOSPITAL IN NEW ORLEANS?—NO!

M. E. Dodd once said, "The story which Jesus told of the Good Samaritan and the admonition he gave with it—'Go thou and do likewise'—defines the duty of every Christian and every Christian denomination. It is their duty to minister to the bodies as well as to the souls of men. Jesus set them the example by healing, teaching, and praying."

When Dr. Dodd was a young pastor and went as a messenger to the Southern Baptist Convention at Jacksonville, Florida, he was thrown into a heated debate. The issue before that convention was whether to establish a Baptist hospital at New Orleans. Hospitals were rather a new venture in Baptist history, and many of the patriarchs of the church opposed the idea as revolutionary and radical. To them the church's scope should be confined to the realm of the spiritual man, and hospitalization or ministering to the physical man, they insisted, belonged to non-religious institutions.

When the proposal to establish the hospital was presented, some of the denomination rose in their might, flailed the air with speech, and condemned it with vigor as an activity beyond the purpose of the denomination. Leaders in this opposition included prominent businessmen, a former candidate for president of the United States on the Prohibition Party ticket, past presidents of the convention, a seminary president, and professors. Nevertheless, the proponents were not without an able champion.

At the request of a caucus of the Louisiana messengers, rose that day a young minister, M. E. Dodd, who led the fight for the hospital with such high-powered, disciplined vigor that when the vote was taken, the project was approved by an overwhelming majority. The Baptist Hospital was built to serve all denominations, those of other faiths, or no faith, and— like the Good Samaritan—those in need. (It served for many years before being sold. The sale of it is still being used today for Baptist Community Ministries.)

They stood and sang "Onward Christian Soldiers"

> Like a mighty army, moves the church of God;
> Brothers we are treading where the saints have trod;
> We are not divided; all one body we,
> One in hope and doctrine, one in charity.

Baptists have always progressed on the heels of different opinions, but when the vote was in, they marched as one.

TEMPLE BAPTIST CHURCH—LOS ANGELES, CALIFORNIA

It was deeply regretted when Dr. Dodd resigned First Baptist Church of Shreveport to accept the pastorate of the three thousand-member Temple Baptist Church in Los Angeles, California, in 1927.

First Church recalled him after he had been there seven months. He wired that he was happy to accept the call and would return at the most opportune moment.

The congregation, overjoyed with the good news, stood applauding and sang, "Praise God From Whom All Blessings Flow."

Dr. Dodd said he would probably have stayed in California, but the Lord led him back because the college needed him. Did you catch that? The Lord led him back after seven months.

Many writers and pastors have said his going to California was a mistake. Some even laughed that even preachers had feet of clay. But Dr. Dodd told me himself that he prayed for weeks before he went and knew God wanted him to go. What we think is man's mistake is the Master's making. This was the beginning of Southern Baptists sowing seeds across America.

EVANGELISM

Dr. Dodd felt strongly about evangelism, and in the tract "Southern Baptist Evangelism" he wrote of its importance.

> **Evangelism has made Southern Baptists what they are and Evangelism must sustain them to the end.** Every Baptist, every church, every organization, agency, institution, minister and missionary are the result of evangelism. If Baptists are to have churches, institutions, missionaries, ministers and members in the future, they must win people to Christ today. Other reli-

gious groups can live by other means, but not Baptists. Baptists have no earthly altar or sacrament. The center and symbol of their ministry is a pulpit, an open Bible, and a divinely called and sent man of God proclaiming the gospel. If Baptists would continue to grow, they must glow and go with the gospel.

When Baptists cease to magnify the proclamation of the gospel as their primary task, they begin to die. Baptists, therefore cannot successfully use the plans or methods of others. When Baptists make the inevitable sacrifices or compromises in order to imitate others, they always lose ground.

It has been the sense of destiny, of missions and of message which have made Southern Baptists great. A continuation of this conviction will bring bigger conquests yet.

The "Southern Baptist Evangelism" tract was distributed all over the world. In 1945 when Southern Baptists engaged in their Centennial Evangelistic Crusade, they asked Dr. Dodd to lead them in this great soul-winning effort, and the First Church graciously released their pastor for a full year.

That year saw Dr. Dodd shuttling back and forth between the far-flung borders of the Southern Baptist Convention, organizing, speaking, inspiring, and leading Southern Baptists in one of their greatest efforts to win the lost.

FIRST BAPTIST CHURCH—SHREVEPORT, LOUISIANA

I came once again to Travis and McNeil. Where are you, old church? Where are the stones . . . the grandeur . . . the beauty? Now, nothing but this historic plaque to say that you were here. Located outside an office building now on the site, the plaque reads:

The First Baptist Church in Shreveport, founded on February 14, 1845, moved to its third location at this site on October 11, 1908. The sanctuary was extensively remodeled and a tower constructed in 1922. A Chapel and educational building were added in 1950. Final services were held here on February 5, 1963, after which the congregation relocated on the former Dodd College Campus, Ockley Drive at Highland Avenue.

I asked again, "Where are the stones?" Then, the earth began to rumble, and I could hear a voice thunder forth—breaking the silence saying, "The stones are scattered all over the world. The torch has been passed; continue in this vein, lest

First Baptist Church of Shreveport, Louisiana, stood at the corner of Travis and McNeil Streets from 1908 until 1963. There were Sunday school rooms on every floor of the ten-story tower, a tearoom, and sanctuary seating 3,998.

The interior of the downtown First Baptist Church, Shreveport, was cathedral-like with brass railings, Florentine artistry, chenille carpets, and indirect lighting.

we forget that the church is the people, not towering masses of concrete and steel. Mark 13:1–2 came to mind. As Jesus was leaving the Temple—one of his disciples said, "Teacher, what beautiful buildings these are! Look at the decorated stonework on the walls."

"Yes, look! For not one stone will be left upon another, except as ruins."

Realizing this, I looked up into the heavens, toward our eternal home—the inheritance of the saints. Then I saw the tower rise again and the bells ringing to the ends of the earth. Come visit the great Gothic structure with her ten-story tower which had a Sunday School room on every floor. The top of the tower housed the thirteen bell chimes with a roof garden to accommodate 1,000 people. Other unique amenities were the daily tearoom service which was established to minister to women, and a broadcasting station. Before Bible conferences were prolific, First Church was headquarters for preachers from all over because it had a seating capacity of 3,998. It was Dr. Dodd's base to lift up the name of Christ to our nation and around the world.

As I steal to my desk in the early morn, I go to find the Lord waiting to give me thoughts that warm my heart and, I pray, that invade the inner soul of others. If you have read this far, you probably realize that I have extensive files, books, magazines, and statistics about our denomination. They have been used sparingly—only where I felt it was needed.

The church downtown did not move because it was old. It had been remodeled many times. A magnificent chapel and educational building had been built in 1950—only thirteen years before the church moved. Just briefly, times changed and people never realized that one day a family of five might each come to church in their own car. We had a large parking lot across the street from the church that was leased. The time came when we wanted to buy, and the owners knew why. The price was astronomical, even for a healthy church budget. There was no choice but to move, but where? God had a place waiting.

DODD COLLEGE

One of the ideals of Dodd College was "Liberty without license; freedom without fanaticism; self-control without self-disparagement; self-expression without flippancy; self-criticism without self-pity." The college opened its doors in 1927 and closed in 1942. Dr. Dodd did not want the school named after him, but the board insisted and felt even stronger when he left to go to California.

At the time of the founding of Dodd College, the Dodds lived at 601 Ockley Drive in Shreveport, Louisiana (above). In 1982, the home was placed on the Historic Register. Medjoy is now owned by Mr. and Mrs. Hubert Joyner, Dr. Dodd's granddaughter and her husband.

A book has been written on this subject, *Dodd College in Shreveport* by Dr. Stan A. Wilkins in 1988. Yes, God did have a place waiting for First Baptist Church. The campus of Dodd College in all its beauty was ideal for the new imposing citadel which was built there—the church in all its strength would continue its mission. The books say that Dodd College closed in 1942, but it really never closed. God was in this from the very beginning. Dodd College was waiting.

Centenary College of Shreveport bought the property, then later, the Baptists bought it back from the Methodists, bringing their diamonds and gold to take back what was dear to them. However, God's secret plan was revealed when real estate builders wanted to buy the property to showcase exclusive homes. There was a clause in the deed that said this property could only be used for Christian education. Dodd College never closed!

CHAPTER 8

Tracts on Track

DR. DODD'S CONVICTIONS AND THEOLOGY WERE TRULY ON track as he blazed an unprecedented trail with the flow of his pen. The voracious reader and prolific writer authored fifteen books and forty-seven tracts and pamphlets; some of which have crossed the seas and been translated into seven different languages with a total circulation of over eight million. Such a quantity might seem quite the norm today, but his copyrights are from 1917, the 1920s, 1930s, and they continued until he died. There were even reprints after his passing. When you consider the subject of his writings, Jesus Christ — the same yesterday, today, and forever — is it any wonder? Embracing sacred themes, Dr. Dodd's tracts were partisan — bearing strong loyalty to a cause. That is why he always used the word *tract*, for there never has been a more worthwhile cause! He knew they would leave an indelible mark on the heart of the reader. There was no danger of derailment — they were all on track.

His most famous tract, "Safe If Saved," was his first. "A Call Comes Ringing" reveals the first fruits of the young pastor's pen while serving in Fulton, Kentucky. He thought, "I am trying to win others to Christ and have not convinced my own father of his need for Christ." So he sent his father the tract which stirred his heart and brought about his salvation.

Papa Dodd was a fine man — a good man — with great strength of character. Sound familiar? He was a good man, but he had never accepted Christ as his Lord and Savior. Thus follows the tract that spoke to his father and traveled all over the world:

Safe If Saved: A Bible Reading
by M. E. Dodd

Can a child of God backslide so far as to be finally lost?
Neither opinion nor observation can answer this question. They do not

have full information. To prove final apostasy one must show, beyond a doubt, one of two things:

1) That the one lost had really been saved; or,

2) That the one saved was actually lost.

The Bible, and the Bible alone, can settle this matter. "All Scripture is given by inspiration of God, and is profitable for doctrine, for instruction in righteousness" (2 Tim. 3:16). "To the word and to the testimony" (Isa. 8:20). "What sayeth the Scriptures?" (Rom. 4:3). "Ye do err, not knowing the Scriptures" (Matt. 22:29). Let us "reason out the Scriptures," and "search the Scriptures" (John 5:39). In so doing we shall be "more noble" (Acts 17:11) than others, and also shall "through comfort of the Scriptures have hope" (Rom. 15:4), "and light" (Ps. 119:130), "and wisdom" (Ps. 19:7), "and faith" (John 20:31), "and joy." (Ps. 19:8).

What do the Scriptures teach regarding the safety of a saved soul? First, the Scriptures teach that the saved soul is surely safe because it is dependent for safety upon Him who is able to keep it.

1) 1 Peter 4:19, "Wherefore let them . . . commit the keeping of their souls to Him in well doing, as unto a faithful Creator." When one commits the keeping of his soul to God, then responsibility for his soul's safety passes to God. Money deposited in a bank is as safe as the vault and the financial strength of the bank. Just so the soul committed to God is as safe as the omnipotent power of God Almighty.

2) Colossians 3:3, "For . . . your life is hid with Christ in God." The bosom of the Almighty is the resting place of the believer. There, he is surely safe until some uncreated monster arises and drives a dagger of death into the heart of God, and lifts a flag of victory over the grave of Jesus Christ.

3) 1 Peter 1:5, the saved are "kept by the power of God, through faith unto Salvation ready to be revealed in the last time." It is God's power and not man's that does the keeping. "But," answers one, "it says 'through faith' and faith can be lost." Faith cannot be destroyed except by a change in the person in whom faith is reposed. Therefore, when faith is once reposed in Jesus Christ it can never be lost, for He is, "The same yesterday, and today, and forever" (Heb. 13:8).

4) 2 Timothy 1:12, "I know whom" not "*in* Whom," (as many quote it), but "whom I have believed, and am persuaded that He is able to keep that which I have committed unto Him against that day." Surely, God, who is able to save a soul, is able to keep it saved.

We believe in a God who is not only able, but who is both willing and determined because He is both faithful and loyal to His covenant. Let others trust whom or what they will, our trust is in Him "whose counsel standeth forever" (Ps. 33:11); who "changes not" (Mal. 3:6); "with whom is

William Henry Dodd (pictured above) was the father of M. E. Dodd. Shown standing in front of Dodd College, the elder Dodd was won to the Lord by reading his son's first tract.

no variation, neither shadow that is cast by turning" (James 1:17, RSV): "the same yesterday, and today, and forever" (Heb. 13:8).

We have committed our souls to Him who says: "Fear thou not, for I am with thee, be not dismayed, for I am thy God! I will strengthen thee, yea, I will uphold thee with the right hand of my righteousness," (Isa. 41:10).

Second, the Scriptures teach that there is no created thing in heaven, earth, or hell that can destroy a child of God or take him away from God.

1) Satan cannot destroy the child of God because "he that is begotten of God, keepeth himself, and that wicked one toucheth him not" (1 John 5:18). Satan may destroy his property or his health as he did Job's "only upon himself put not forth thine hand," (Job 1:12), saith Jehovah.

2) Sin cannot destroy the child of God, because "sin shall not have dominion over you" (Rom. 6:14). Sin may have influence over God's child, but cannot have dominion. Sin is not the reigning power in his life, Christ is his Lord and Master.

3) Temptation cannot destroy the child of God, because "there hath no temptation taken you but such as is common to man; but God is faithful, who will not suffer you to be tempted above that ye are able, but will with the temptation also make a way to escape that ye may be able to bear it" (1 Cor. 10:13).

4) The world cannot destroy the child of God because: "whatsoever is born of God overcometh the world," (1 John 5:4).

5) The saved man cannot destroy himself, because: God says, "I will make an everlasting covenant with them, that I will not turn away from them to do them good; but I will put my fear in their hearts, that they shall not depart from me" (Jer. 32:40).

6) Tribulation, or distress, or persecution, or famine, or nakedness, or peril, or sword cannot destroy the child of God, because "in all these things we are more than conquerors through Him that loved us" (Rom. 8:35, 37). What it means to be more than conqueror, one cannot say. That is language too high for one whose feet are tied to the earth. One must soar into the third heaven and hear things unlawful to be spoken (2 Cor. 12) to get an idea of what it means to be "more than conqueror through Him who loved us." We can only understand that it is intended to teach that somewhere, somehow, sometime, the child of God shall be brought to his home, at last "through many dangers, toils, and snares," a triumphant victor; waving his palm of victory (Rev. 7:9) over death, hell, and the grave.

7) No other created thing can destroy the child of God, because "I am persuaded that neither death, nor life, nor angels, nor principalities, nor powers, nor things present, nor things to come, nor height, nor depth, nor any other creature [created thing] shall be able to separate us from the love of God which is in Christ Jesus our Lord" (Rom. 8:38–39).

Third, the Scriptures teach that the nature of salvation is such as to prevent it from ever being changed.

1) Saved persons are elected and predestinated to salvation "According as He hath chosen us in Him before the foundation of the world . . . having predestinated us unto the adoption of children by Jesus Christ to Himself according to the good pleasure of His will" (Eph. 1:4–6).

2) Saved persons are regenerated. "Except a man be born again he cannot see the Kingdom of God. Ye must be born again" (John 3:3, 7). In nature, the relation of parent and child cannot be changed. Much less can it be changed in grace. One cannot be unborn.

3) Saved persons are children of God. They are not servants with a relation to the Master dependent upon works, but they are children having a relation as unchangeable as the nature of God (Gal. 4:7). "For ye are all the children of God by faith in Christ Jesus" (Gal. 3:26). "But as many as received Him, to them gave He power to become the sons of God" (John 1:12). Think you that God's Son shall ever sink into hell?

4) Saved persons have eternal life. This is declared 43 times in John's gospel alone. Some of the most familiar of these passages are John 3:14, 16, 36; 5:24; 10:28 — "Everlasting life," "Eternal life," "hath everlasting life." "I give unto them eternal life." Note the present tense of the verbs "hath" and "give." The salvation of the soul is spoken of in the Scriptures as a present possession. Now, if it is eternal life and a present possession, when will the possessor ever lose it? Not until eternity ends. If the experience he has, and thinks of as salvation, comes to an end, and he is lost, it was not eternal. If eternal, he will never lose it.

5) Saved persons are not now condemned (Rom. 8:1); "There is therefore, now, no condemnation to them which are in Christ Jesus," (John 3:18); "He that believeth in Him is not condemned" (John 5:25).

6) Saved persons never shall be condemned. "He that heareth my word and believeth on Him that sent me hath everlasting life and shall not come into condemnation" (John 5:24). Certainly, if the child of God is not now condemned, nor ever shall be, then there is no probability, not even a possibility, that he shall ever be lost.

7) Saved persons have been saved by the grace of God (Eph. 2:8-9). "For, by grace are ye saved through faith; and that not of yourselves; it is the gift of God; not of works, lest any man should boast."

Salvation is a work of God's grace done once and for all, never to be done over, never to be undone.

Fourth, the Scriptures teach that God's character and Christ's work are such as to guarantee eternal salvation to those who trust Him. "Yea, I have loved thee with an everlasting love" (Jer. 31:3).

God's eternal character is pledged to the eternal safety of God's child.

If God loses one soul He loses His honor, and in that case there can be no assurance that He can save any. If the devil can get any of God's children, and does not, then those whom He does not get are saved by the disgrace of the devil and not by the grace of God.

"But what is to be done with the Christian who sins?" one asks. God's character of spotless holiness will not allow Him to condone or palliate sin, not even in His child. But, does God send His child to hell for sin?" No! He says "If His children forsake my law and walk not in my judgments; if they break my statutes and keep not my commandments; then will I visit their transgression with the rod, and their iniquity with stripes" (Ps. 89:30). God will chastise the disobedient or wayward child like a loving Father but He will not cast him off forever. "Nevertheless, my loving kindness will I not utterly take from him nor suffer my faithfulness to fail" (Ps. 89:33).

We have been saved and are safe because Christ "gave Himself for us that He might redeem us from all iniquity" (Titus 2:14). "Jesus paid it all." "The wages of sin is death" (Rom. 6:23), and "Christ died for our sins" (1 Cor. 15:3). Now, God's character being what it is, He cannot and will not collect from my substitute, Jesus Christ who died in my stead, for my sins, and then collect from me too. God said He was satisfied with Christ's death (Isa. 53). When we accept Christ as our Saviour, then God accepts us. If God should reject a saved person, He would be rejecting Jesus, His Son.

Christ's work was, and is, intercessory as well as sacrificial and substitutionary, (John 17:11). "Holy Father, keep through thine own name those whom Thou hast given me." Will God, the Father, hear and answer this prayer of His only begotten and well beloved Son? Christ Himself said, "Father, I thank Thee that Thou hast heard me, and I knew that Thou hearest me always," (John 11:41–42). Now, if the Father hears Christ always, then this prayer "keep" was heard, and God will do what His Son asked Him. He will "keep those whom thou hast given me."

Verse 20, "Neither pray I for these alone, but for them also which shall believe on me through their word." It is a blessed thought that our Saviour looked down the long vistas of time and saw all of the wayward, thoughtless stumbling children of God in all the ages and prayed for them, "Holy Father, KEEP them." Not only did He pray for them while on earth, but He prays for them now in heaven (Rom. 8:34). "It is Christ that died, yea, rather that is risen again; who is even at the right hand of God, who also maketh intercession for us" (Heb. 7:25). "Wherefore He is able to save them to the uttermost that come unto God by Him, seeing He ever liveth to make intercession for them" (1 John 2:1). "And if any man sin, we have an advocate with the Father, Jesus Christ, the righteous."

It is a glorious thing to have friends, and loved ones, who pray for us. What a blessing beyond measure to have an affectionate wife, a loving mother and devoted children to pray for us. Far better than all of these, is it, to have a loving Saviour plead our cause at the throne of God.

Five bleeding wounds He bears,
Received on Calvary,
For me, they pour effectual prayers:
Forgive! O, forgive! they cry,
Nor let that ransomed sinner die.

Conclusion

Saved and safe is a glorious doctrine of the word of God and a grand experience for a child of God.

It brings God's children in humility before their Father; it increases their desire to live a pure life and to render obedient service; it brightens their hope, strengthens their faith, and quickens their zeal.

There is no comfort in the fear of being lost. One who is in perpetual fear of falling away is bound to be unhappy and unfitted for service. But there is infinite comfort, consolation and inspiration in the truth of God's Holy Word that we are saved once and for all, never to be done over, and never to be undone. "Blessed be the God and Father of our Lord Jesus Christ."

If you are saved you are safe. You may doubt it occasionally and may be anxious about it. But you are just as safe as the one who has full assurance. Two persons are on a ship in a storm. One is frightened, the other is not worried at all. But they are equally safe, because their safety is in the ship and not in their feelings.

All who are saved are equally safe though they may not believe it or understand it. Safety is in Him who died for our sins and in whom the believer trusts. We are as safe as Christ is sure.

Fear not, I am with thee; Oh be not dismayed;
I, I am thy God and will still give thee aid;
I'll strengthen thee, help thee, and cause thee to stand,
Upheld by my righteous, omnipotent hand.

The soul that on Jesus hath leaned for repose
I will not, I will not desert to his foes;
That soul though all hell should endeavor to shake,
I'll never, no never, no never, forsake.

Benediction

Jude 24–25: "Now unto Him that is able to *keep you from falling*, and to present you faultless before the presence of His glory with exceeding joy, to the only wise God, our Saviour, be glory and majesty, dominion and power, both now and ever, Amen."

CAST A LOOK AT THE TRAIL OF TRACTS BY DR. DODD

"Southern Baptist Evangelism"
"The Spirit Filled Life"
"The Virtue of Vision"
"The Lord's Day"
"23 Reasons Why I Tithe and Teach Tithing"
"Christ the Son of the Living God"
"How to Know and Do the Will of God"
"God's Financial Plan"
"How the Burial of Christ Saves from Sin"

Such a trail of tracts would turn the strongest left to the right. When Dr. and Mrs. Dodd girdled the globe for God in 1934, it was quite clear that music was the speech of angels—an international language. Beyond the seas on foreign soil, newspaper headlines and pictures revealed that his tracts in their language broke all barriers. It was a drenching melody—

"Como Comenzor a Diezmar"
por M. E. Dodd

"Como Tener Exito (en La Vida Christiano)"
por El Dr. Monroe E. Dodd

"Seguro, Se Salvo"
por M. E. Dodd

I didn't grow up with tracts and at times haven't cared for being handed one. But after opening up my heart to these—Father, forgive me. Many are starving to look inside and find Jesus. One magazine expressed its support with this statement, "Dr. Dodd's tracts have contributed great service to the denomination." May we follow in this train and stay on track.

CHAPTER 9

"Money given to the church and the Cooperative Program will go farther, rise higher, spread wider, work deeper, and last longer than when given to any other place or cause."

— M. E. Dodd —

Sacred How

•

A PIERCING SOUND OF A GAVEL MEETING THE HARD SURFACE of the podium rang out to call the messengers of the 1925 Southern Baptist Convention meeting in Memphis, Tennessee, to order.

Let's turn the clock back even more and listen to the echoes of the past which have made possible the music of today. It is 1919 — Convention time — Baptists need money. "We must raise fifty million dollars," said some; but, after challenges by Dodd, and other leaders who believed the goal to be too low, they voted to raise the goal to seventy-five million dollars. Thus, the Seventy-five Million Dollar Campaign was launched! It was a five year program, 1919–1924.

Dr. Dodd gave of his time during the next five years to travel through the southern states speaking at every turn of the tour to use his influence to arouse Baptists because of need; when you need, you dare!

This is tremendous faith. As the campaign drew to a close, our leaders realized a stable plan must be worked out where all agencies and causes of the denomination would be granted an adequate and fair share of the funds received by the convention. A committee was appointed. Dr. Dodd was named chairman to investigate methods of distributing money and asked to make a report at the next convention.

The Cooperative Program was not fortuitous — God came and spoke to His chosen man. "History is shaped by individuals," they say, and God always speaks to one person to lead His people. The Lord came to Monroe Elmon in a dream. He was standing in a field — the wind was blowing, and it was not harnessed — powerful like the Holy Spirit. "I can hear the music," Dr. Dodd told the Lord, "but there is a major note missing. How, Lord? How? Tell me how, Lord?" There was silence like the lull after a clap of thunder. "I will be with you when you present it to the Southern

Baptist Convention. It will not be easy, but the passing of it will be a sign that I am with you. Go to your people, they will listen." When the time came, Dr. Dodd gave the report; then, he bravely remained on the platform to face a barrage of questions. For half an hour, the questions came, and he answered them. When they were through discussing it, the convention voted to adopt it. God never forgets those who call upon Him—the Cooperative Program was presented in 1925, and there was not one dissenting vote.

> The Cooperative Program is intercession in behalf of all our great causes which Christ has committed to our trust. We believe that Southern Baptists should go forward together year by year in high and holy endeavor until His kingdom shall stretch from shore to shore, and His name shall be known from the river to the ends of the earth.
>
> —M. E. Dodd, Chairman

As one history of Baptists reveals—the Cooperative Program ranks as one of the most telling contributions of M. E. Dodd to kingdom causes. Little could they realize that day how far reaching the significance of their actions.

With such a positive vote, one would have expected the program to be an immediate success. Not so! Dr. Dodd said, "Baptists have disagreed, but always come together in the end for a greater need. The cause of Jesus Christ was above all."

Through the years, giants of the faith, from one end of our land to another, have lifted their voices: "It is a Jesus program. Millions of Southern Baptists are pooling their resources for one purpose—to advance the cause of Christ."

"God gave us our marching orders to take the gospel into all the world."

"We are unapologetically committed to winning people to Jesus Christ. That's our only reason for being!"

Dr. Dodd himself said, "Money given to the church and the Cooperative Program will go Farther, Rise Higher, Spread Wider, Work Deeper, and Last Longer than when given to any other place or cause."

Young people and young ministers that do not know our roots are not aware that what Baptists have today, great hearts of the faith have fought, bled, and died for all kingdom causes. We have benefited by those who have gone before us. Will those who come after us benefit? Or, will they be denied because we have forgotten our mission and wherewithal to advance the kingdom of God's leadership? So, through the years, when some of our young hearts have asked, "Are they trying to make a Sacred Cow out of the

Dr. Dodd was the leader of the Million Prayers Daily–Million Souls Saved program.

Cooperative Program?" Many greats across our land have said, "No! It's not a Sacred Cow, it's a Sacred *How!*" Glory to God in the Highest!

Our Cooperative Program sends out a wave of influence that is felt around the world. Missionaries have touched hundreds that have been led to a spiritual knowledge of our Lord. These new believers in turn escorted others from the threshold of unbelief to the gates of eternal life.

When Southern Baptists established the Cooperative Program in 1925, the denomination became the largest single international missions-sending agency in world Protestantism. Someone had lighted the way, and the path, while not clear, was less rocky; for a faint light twinkled in the distance, and beckoned Southern Baptists.

World War I was over, and another on its way; but we were also at war against satanic forces. This was one way we could march to the beat of Christian intellect and arm our youth with the ammunition of the young Prince of Peace.

This was D Day . . . the bugle had sounded, and there would be no retreat! Southern Baptists had landed on another beachhead. . . .

A piano tuner crossed my path today. He was attempting to enlighten me since it was obvious that I did not have a natural ear for music. "Piano tuning works this way," he said. "There is a four-forty over A. If you start with that, every other element in the octave is just a little off from A to forty-four. They call it a chromatic scale, a well-tempered scale." Everyone is a little imperfect, but they were designed to make a well-connected scale. Together you can have harmony. Do you hear the notes as they play in harmony? Around the world, hearts are singing—hearts rejoicing in the warmth of our Savior's love because a living giant we call the Cooperative Program was conceived in the mind of a giant of the faith.

It began as a small clapper inside the great bell; but now, the sound reverberates literally girdling the globe for God. The Cooperative Program is the largest "bell" ever cast by Southern Baptists—silent until the clapper strikes a chord and the chimes sound round the world. Each Southern Baptist is a clapper and only we can keep the bell ringing. We must pull the ropes of the past to ring the bells of the future.

Chapter 10

1925

TURN THE KNOB ON YOUR RADIO TO 1925, AND THERE WILL be a shadow of the past: "Sweet Georgia Brown," . . . "If you knew Susie, like I know Susie," . . . yes, a tidal wave of remembrance comes forth shimmering on the expanding rim of memory.

"Five Foot Two—Eyes of Blue" and the melancholy chords of "Moonlight and Roses." You call to your son to go get a gallon of milk and hand him fifty-six cents. No—wait! You don't have to go—the milkman comes to the door, but we do need a loaf of bread—here's nine cents!

In 1925, John Scopes was teaching the theory of evolution in the Tennessee public schools. Since this was contrary to state law, he was arrested.

William Jennings Bryan assisted the prosecution, and Scopes was defended by Clarence Darrow. The great orator and statesman Bryan won the case for the state, and Scopes was fined one hundred dollars. The newspapers rang out—Scopes Found Guilty in Tennessee's "Monkey Trial." In that same year and state, the Southern Baptists adopted the Cooperative Program at the convention in Memphis.

It was the beginning of Baptist sowing seeds farther, higher, wider, and deeper than they had ever done before to tell the world about Jesus. Now, seventy-five years later, the newspapers remind us of our history with one news release after another, celebrating the program's anniversary.

Since 1925, Southern Baptists have given nearly ten billion dollars through the Cooperative Program to support over 6,000 North American missionaries and almost 5,000 international missionaries, to educate 140,000 seminary students, to start thousands of new churches, to fund countless benevolent and relief ministries, and to underwrite a whole array of other Christian endeavors. (The numbers are constantly increasing, but at the time of this printing, these figures were correct.)

Dr. and Mrs. Dodd in his office at First Baptist Church, Shreveport. They traveled the globe together fulfilling the mission of the Cooperative Program which Dr. Dodd pioneered.

The Southern Baptist Convention celebrated the seventy-fifth birthday of the Cooperative Program at their meeting in Orlando, Florida, on June 13, 2000. The Cooperative Program Executive Committee presented the M. E. Dodd Award to Dr. Jim Henry, pastor of First Baptist Church in Orlando.

The award was named for M. E. Dodd in honor of his conception of the idea of cooperative giving among churches and presentation of the plan to the convention in Memphis in 1925, calling this plan the "safest, sanest, and most scriptural way to finance our Kingdom work." The trophy is a beautiful, cast-bronze piece, approximately twelve inches in diameter, which depicts a man walking on top of the world sowing seeds for the Lord.

The trophy truly reflects the heart and mind of Dr. Dodd's ministry, for he kept a world globe on his desk. While visiting with individuals in his office, he would often place his hand on the globe, indicating an affinity for missions which kept him in tune with God who led him to the far corners of the earth.

On hand for the presentation were Dodd descendants—granddaughter Virginia Joyner, great granddaughter Emilane Watson and great-great grandchildren, Jared and Alaena Watson.

In accepting the award, Henry paid homage to Dodd and to all of those who have supported the Cooperative Program.

"This is for Dr. Dodd and our spiritual forefathers who had heart and vision to fulfill what God had for the Southern Baptist Convention in diagramming the most magnificent way to reach the world for Christ," Henry said.

It was June of 1989—I was visiting my daughter and her family in Troutdale, Oregon, where God had sent them to build a church in the great Northwest. My daughter Darlene wanted me to see Multnomah Falls in all its splendor. It is the second highest falls in the United States (620 feet) and is located 30 miles east of Portland in the beautiful breathtaking Columbia River Gorge.

The Columbia River is vast and wide, reaching as far as the eye can see. There was no doubt that this was God's handiwork. The falls were cascading over the cliff, trees, and rocks, ending up in a quiet rock pool, which moved slowly on to the Columbia River. I picked up a shiny pebble, threw it into the water, and it made little silver circles with a rippling melody over the water. As they kept going out . . . out . . . and out, modeling their musical faith, I thought of all the waves of influence from hundreds who have literally gone into every part of the world to light a path for a world in darkness without Jesus Christ.

"Do the falls ever stop flowing?" I asked.

"No," my daughter answered, "except when it freezes. That only happens when there is a drop in temperature and a strong wind blowing through the gorge with no moisture in the air."

I had a look on my face that prompted her to question me.

"Mother, what's wrong?"

"The falls remind me of the Cooperative Program—we must never let it freeze—it must never stop flowing!"

Heroes of the faith bled and died for what is ours today. Since 1925, the Cooperative Program has provided a way for Southern Baptists to carry the torch of the Lord Jesus Christ and has set hearts aflame in every nation by taking the hands of the unsaved and leading them into the halls of eternity.

Let us pass the torch—not drop it! If we drop it, we will have ashes instead of a fire. We must continue to run the race til the Lord comes again.

CHAPTER 11

Half Notes

M. E. DODD'S PEN RANG THE CLARION BELLS OF GLORY WITH fifteen books from the houses of publishers Broadman, William B. Eerdman, Fleming H. Revell, and others that encouraged him to keep the ink flowing. Here are some nuggets of grace. They can become your constant companion—an intellectual treasure trove in your life.

As I looked through Dr. Dodd's books, I thought, "These have a lot of years on them." Then I felt a wind that rustled the pages, and I heard a locomotive, an iron courser, stamping titanic hooves upon my heart, and it hit me. No matter the dates of these copyrights—1917, 1927, 1929, 1930, 1934—the message of the Lord Jesus Christ was the same yesterday as today. Moisture came to my eyes, for I realized these words were being read and preached before most of us reading this were born—"Read on—it's forever!"

It is an unchanging gospel!

These are not Dr. Dodd's books in their entirety; but pieces on the scale of life—half notes rather than whole notes.

In 1920, these were addresses given to young people at summer assemblies. The Scriptures ascribe one hundred and ten titles to our Lord Jesus Christ. These titles cover all the range of His wonderful personality and His marvelous character.

Jesus, the Lily

"I am the Rose of Sharon and the Lily of the Valley."—Song of Solomon 2:1

Let us walk today into the flower garden of God. We come at once to the lily in all of its purity, beauty, and fragrance. Sitting down beside it we ask, what have you to say for our Lord Jesus Christ? We get our answer immediately.

The lily speaks to us first of all of the purity of Jesus. The purity of the lily makes it the fittest of all flowers for the adornment of the marriage altar and for the softening of the death chamber. At both the nuptial feast and the silent grave, the Lord Jesus ought also always to be present.

So spotless white was the character of Jesus that Pilate was compelled to say: "I find no fault in Him"; and even Judas Iscariot confessed: "I have betrayed innocent blood." So conscious of His own sinless soul was Jesus that He looked His enemies straight in the face and demanded "which one of you convicteth me of sin?" and not a word they spoke.

The lily can grow amidst the miasmatic poison of an impure pond and yet be as spotless as the first morning sunbeams that kiss its dimpled cheek. Thus, Jesus deliberately associated Himself with the poor, the dirty, the immoral, the outcast, but never a taint of their impurity did He contract.

Jesus was the most amazing, the most startling, the most sensational man in character and conduct that the world ever saw.

The Lily of the Valley speaks to us also of the beauty of Jesus. He is the fairest among ten thousand and the one altogether lovely. His was that beauty which differentiates the perfect building of a trained architect from the bungled mass of a crude builder; that distinguishes the finished product of an artistic genius from the dabblings of a mere amateur.

Compare the wild flowers of the fields and woods with the fully developed American Beauty or La France; contrast the gruesome and repulsive vulture whose horrible beak, face, and frazzled feathers come from the carrion upon which he feeds, with the dainty and delicate bird of paradise whose finely spun feathers surpass in beauty the most delicate maidenhair fern. In these contrasts you will see the difference between Jesus of Nazareth whose food was heavenly manna, and whose purity sprang forth in the most beautiful personality the eyes of man ever looked upon, and those repulsive faces and figures in whose lines are written lust and passion, hatred and prejudice, greed and graft.

The beauty of Jesus also possesses that strength and power which belong alone to reality. A mere tacked-on beauty is oftentimes repulsive, but a beauty of soul and a beautiful character which radiates in a beautiful face and figure sit upon a throne before which the world's scepters are piled, and it chooses which it will, and "All orators are dumb when beauty speaks."

Beauty is also possessed of a mighty mission. The beauty of Jesus serves the best of all purposes. It exalts, it inspires, it lifts up, it glorifies. His was not the beauty which is "the fading rainbow's pride." His was the beauty heightened by goodness, sweetened by love, and glorified by service.

Jesus, the Lamb
"Behold the Lamb of God." John 1:29

Jesus as a Lion! Jesus as a Lamb! What a strange contradiction of titles! What strange contrast of characteristics! What manner of man is this in whom are mingled the strength and courage of a lion, the tenderness and timidity of a lamb? Here, in the character and personality of Christ, is the one place where the lion and the lamb lie down together.

The people saw Jesus one day bold and defiant; they heard Him challenge His enemies and scorch them with judgements, and they said: "He is the Lion of the Tribe of Judah." The next day they saw Him move among the sick and the suffering and the sorrowing with the tenderness of a mother, and they said: "He is the Lamb of God." One day they heard Him rebuke the demons with divine authority, and the next day they saw Him caress little children, and they said: "The Lion and the Lamb are met together in His nature."

What lessons has the lamb for us about Jesus? What do you think of when you see a lamb?

As I recall my boyhood days in Tennessee sitting on the hillside of the old farm watching the sheep and the lambs in the meadow, the first thing I think of is the frolicsomeness of the lamb. For sheer joy at being alive the lamb leaped and bounded and gamboled over the meadows.

This joy He was constantly seeking to impart to others. "The fruit of the spirit is love, joy." "That my joy may be in you and your joy may be full." "Rejoice and be exceeding glad." And after He was gone the beloved apostle wrote, "These things write I unto you that your joy may be full." "Rejoice in the Lord alway and again I say rejoice." "The joy of the Lord is your strength."

Who are the happiest faced people you know? Watch the happy faced children, women, and men who come down from the church houses on a glad Sunday morning where they have heard of Jesus. Are they not the very embodiment of His own unspeakable joy?

But was He not a man of sorrows and acquainted with grief? Yes, this is true. But joy and sorrow are not antagonistic. They are [next]door neighbors in the human heart. The parentage of both is the capacity for deep feeling, the sensitiveness which responds readily to the touch of God and the needs of man. And Jesus never lost that unfailing joy even under the shadow of the cross. For is it not written that "For the joy that was set before Him, He endured the cross and looked with contempt upon the shame"?

I visited a great packing plant in Kansas City and saw the slaughter of the animals. I saw the mighty hammer swung by giant arms fall with death blows upon the skull of the cow, and I heard her kick and stamp and bellow. I saw the slaughter of the pigs and their wild rush into the scalding vat, still alive, where they screamed and squealed and fought for life. Then I came to where the lambs and the sheep were led to the slaughter. I saw the great chain fastened around the hind leg of a meek and spotless lamb, and it drew him up until he swung clear. Then I saw the knife plunged into his throat until it struck his heart and the lifeblood gushed out. But not a sound of protest of complaint ever escaped his mouth, not a twitch of a muscle nor the flicker of a nerve. As life slowly ebbed away, his large soft brown eyes looked appealingly at me, but not a word he spoke. The tragedy and pathos of it was heartrending. I had never understood so well before just what the prophet saw in the long vision of the coming Messiah when he said, "He is brought as a lamb to the slaughter, but opened not his mouth."

. . . And without a word of complaint, He won His victory over death, hell, and the grave.

Jesus, the Lion
"The Lion of the tribe of Judah hath prevailed." —Revelation 5:5.

The Scriptures mention over one hundred titles for our Lord. But in this series we are to consider only four: Jesus as the Lily, the Lamb, the Lion, the Lord.

Jesus as a Lion! What a striking and thrilling picture! He is not only represented as a Lion, but as the Lion of the tribe of Judah.

Judah was the foremost tribe of Israel. The emblem on Judah's banner was the figure of a lion. In Israel's marches, Judah always headed the column, and her flag was the first to challenge the enemy. Great consternation no doubt struck the ranks of the enemy many times as the blazing emblem of the lion on Judah's banner flashed in their faces. Now Jesus is the lion of the Lion Tribe. He is the Lion of Lions.

The Courage of Jesus

The figure of a lion is used some 130 times in the Scriptures. When we see a lion, we think first of all of his strength and courage. As a lion Jesus was the most fearless, the most courageous man this world has ever known. He was also constantly exhorting His disciples, "Be not afraid," "Fear not, fear not."

Jesus had great physical courage. He lived out what He taught; "Fear not him who can destroy the body." There was never a moment when the fear of man was before His face.

Jesus faced disease and danger and death with a poise and calmness characteristic only of a courageous soul. Scientists tell us that fear of a certain disease makes one more susceptible to it. Jesus never fell a victim to the ravages of contagious diseases because, of course, He was first of all God in flesh, but from the human standpoint because He was not afraid.

When the soldiers and His enemies came with lanterns and swords and staves seeking Him in the garden, He did not sneak away in craven cowardice, but He calmly faced them and said: "I am the man ye seek." He faced them with that spirit of fearlessness which said take this poor body of mine and do what you will with it, but in spite of your worst, I will live forever.

Jesus had great intellectual courage. He dared to cut across many scholastic theories of His time.

Jesus announced scientific truth far ahead of His day. He said to His disciples, "After I go away I shall come again to this earth. And my instantaneous return will find two in the field, two at the mill getting breakfast and two in bed, and one of each couple will be taken and one left." Now what is the scientific truth in this statement? It is this: The two in the field represent the middle of the day, the two at the mill represent the morning hour and the two in bed, the midnight hour. This means that the earth is round and that by virtue of its relationship to the sun, at the same instant, there are three different hours on the earth's surface. But it was fifteen hundred years after Jesus made this scientific statement of truth before Galileo and Kepler discovered the true theory of the heliocentric system of the universe.

If the scientists of His time had seen the scientific import of this statement, they no doubt would have done as some would-be scientists of today, charge him with ignorance and of being out of harmony with God's natural universe. But when one charges this against Christ or the Bible it is because he either does not know science, or he does not know the Bible, or he may not know either.

Jesus was intellectually courageous enough to do His own thinking and to even think far ahead of the time in which He lived. But more sublime than all else was the moral courage of Jesus. He dared to do right at whatever cost. There was iron in His blood and steel in His nerves. He had rather die than to yield one hair's breadth of His ideals or principles. To be Christlike is to be lionlike, strong and courageous.

It requires an extraordinarily high type of courage for one to say to his bosom companion, "I cannot even for the sake of your friendship walk in the path that is not God's will." Many a young man and young woman have failed right here. May God give us the courage of Christ, the courage to walk in the way of His will for our life.

The courage of Jesus manifests itself in His bold attacks upon wrongdoers and His enemies. He came into the house of God and saw the profiteers buying and selling and getting gain off of the religious convictions of the people. His heart boiled with indignation at this unholy thing and at this desecration of His Father's house. And He seized a whip of cords and rushing upon them, He kicked over their table, upset their money pots, and lashed the thieves out. Jesus was the most sensational religious teacher the world ever saw. Imagine the hubbub that must have gone on in Jerusalem after this incident.

At the last, when He faced His enemies who were hounding Him to His death, He pointed His finger straight into their faces and said: "Woe unto thee, woe unto thee, ye compass land and sea to make one proselyte and when he is made, he is two-fold more the child of hell than yourselves," and "ye are of your father the devil." Jesus was too much of a gentleman to ever say one hard or unkind word against an unfortunately fallen man or woman. He never once uttered a harsh word toward such. But upon these false accusers, these self righteous and pharisaical hypocrites, He hurled anathemas in biting sarcasm and blistering cynicism until they scorched with the very fires of judgement.

His courage is at its highest in His loyal obedience to the will and word of God. No inducement from His friends, no threat of His enemies, no hope of reward, nor fear of loss could divert Him one hair's breadth from that plan which had been mapped out for Him by His Father from all eternity. To do the will of God was the chief end of His life. It was his bread and meat.

I have seen those with His own lionlike courage, filling their hearts, driven from home and family, ostracized, criticized, and disinherited but notwithstanding all, abiding steadfastly by the will of God. There is no courage more glorious than this.

Jesus, the Lord

"That at the name of Jesus every knee shall bow, of things in heaven, and things in earth, and things under the earth; and that every tongue should confess that Jesus Christ is Lord to the glory of God."—Philippians 2:10–11.

Liberty and Lordship! What apparently incongruous terms. How can one be free and at the same time be subject to an over lordship? How can we as Christians, "Stand fast in the liberty wherewith Christ hath made us free," and at the same time be absolutely amendable to His Lordship in everything?

We had as well ask how the railroad locomotive can be free and at the same time confined to the narrow limits of two rails. It is free only when it is thus confined. The moment it rebels against this limitation and leaps off the rails, it immediately becomes a hopeless and helpless thing. The justice and righteousness of God in Jesus Christ are the two rails upon which the locomotives of human life must run, if they are to be free indeed.

Acknowledgment of the Lordship of Jesus must be voluntary and not coerced. The expression Paul uses, "confess that Jesus is Lord," indicates this distinction. The word is translated in Matthew 11:26, "I thank Thee." It means to voluntarily acknowledge with adoring wonder and holy acquiescence the rightness of the thing proclaimed.

This subject of the Lordship of Jesus brings before us at once the question of the center of authority in religion. There is wide disagreement as to what the center of authority is, as to what the court of final appeal in matters religious is.

There are those who say that conscience is the seat of all authority in religion. They quote with much satisfaction that we are to worship God according to the dictates of our own conscience. All who claim this fail, in the first place, to recognize the proper function of conscience. Conscience is not a dictator. Conscience does not legislate nor administrate. Conscience is only the judge upon the bench who pronounces judgment according to the light he has. *So, unless conscience is enlightened by the Word of God and vitalized by the spirit of God and its judgments are according to the will of God, they are likely to be and most generally are imperfect and quite often very wrong.* We need to learn that it is possible to be perfectly conscientious and yet wrong. The heathen mother who throws her child to the crocodiles or who puts her helpless infant in the arms of a white hot Moloch until its flesh is burned to a crisp does so in all good conscience. Conscience did not dictate this act, but did approve because this was its standard of right. Christians may be conscientious in the performance of religious rites or ceremonies or in the doing of what they consider duty and yet be wrong. *So, one cannot depend upon conscience unless it squares with the high standard found in Christ Jesus.*

Besides all of this, one who sets up in himself the seat of authority in matters religious becomes at once a spiritual anarchist and Bolshevik. *Conscience, to be dependable, must be enlightened by the Holy Spirit and empowered by the Holy Christ.*

Jesus is Lord in the moral kingdom. He changes the very hearts and lives of men and of nations. The pierced hands of this peasant carpenter have lifted empires off their hinges. The glory of England and America today is the glory of Jesus. Fifteen hundred years ago our ancestors were drinking blood out of the skulls of their fathers while China was then an ancient civilization.

Today the Stars and Stripes and the Union Jack cemented by the blood of Flanders Fields into an undying friendship, stand, the world around, as the symbols of justice and righteousness and service. *But it will be only as long as Christ is recognized by these peoples as Lord and Master.*

A brilliant English lady lay dying in Paris during the great exposition there. In a weakened state, she gasped to her friends the one word, "Bring." They, supposing she desired food, brought some, but she shoved it aside and gasped again, "Bring." They brought the most luscious fruit that could be found, but she would have none of it. She said, "Bring." They gathered all of her friends about her, thinking that would satisfy her. Then looking around about, and in clear resonant voice she said:

> Bring forth the royal diadem,
> And crown Him Lord of all.

This coronation hymn is the national anthem of the Kingdom of God. One Sunday morning when our choir was singing an anthem and was mounting up to the full chorus with the organ's full diapason and the grand swell opened, they swung in the midst of it into:

> All hail the power of Jesus' name,
> Let angels prostrate fall.
> Bring forth the royal diadem
> And crown Him Lord of all.

I instinctively rose to my feet and stood at attention, as a British soldier would when he hears the cry, "Soldiers, the King." I said to my people, I shall never again sit while this national anthem of the Kingdom of God is being sung. *He is Lord of Lords and King of Kings forever.*

THE STOCK MARKET CRASH OF 1929 SENT SHOCK WAVES through the American financial community and ruin to thousands of investors. Many minds could not respond except jumping from buildings to their deaths.

Factories and stores shut down. It was 1933, the height of the Great Depression. Poverty swept through the nation on a scale never before experienced. Many people were hungry and stood in bread lines and went to soup kitchens to get food.

On the brink of disaster, a dark silence set in and our countrymen were sitting in the shadow of death; it was their hour of trial. Franklin Delano Roosevelt, our president in 1933, said of the Depression, "These dark days will be worth all they cost us if they teach us that our true destiny is not to be ministered unto but to minister to ourselves and to our fellow men."

The stock market crash and the Depression have nothing to do with Dr. Dodd's book, *Concerning the Collection*, except that is was published in 1929. However, it says volumes about him and Southern Baptists. In the crossroads of the valley of misfortune there were shattering blows and there was knock-down ruination; yet, great hearts had the faith to key in on giving and Stewardship. They could not sit in the shadow of death—this hour of trial—when their Bibles read, "For even the Son of man came not to be ministered unto but to minister, and to give his life a ransom for many."

So, with dollars gone in a flash across our nation and the world, Dr. Dodd wrote a book on stewardship for pastors. It gave them a story and a prayer to use before the collection of tithes and offerings for every Sunday in the year. *Concerning the Collection* was down to earth and practical. Thus, Dr. Dodd was called the Depression president of Southern Baptists, 1933–1935.

This helps us to understand even more why, whenever God's money was needed for God's work, they always called on M. E. Dodd to lead them. He always got to the heart of the person before the heart of the pocketbook. He made you feel—"Let them see the land, not with their eyes, but their hearts."

Dr. Dodd received high praise for *Concerning the Collection.*

The offering in a church, is part of its worship. It should be dignified and serious but not stiff and solemn. In announcing the offering, some pastors play the clown. Others, anathematize long-suffering people. Still others, look as if a smile were a crime. Just what to do, and how to do it, is a problem with many a hard-driven pastor. This book tells how the collection ought to be taken. What pastor will not count such a book a Godsend?

Curtis Lee Laws
The Watchman Examiner
New York City

Concerning the Collection

The highest aim in asking for the church offering, is not to get money but to secure the consecration of manhood; not coin, but character; not talents of clanking silver, but talents of mastered manhood.

With the conviction that the handling of money for the Master, in both its getting and giving, should be taken out of the realm of emotionalism and placed in that of a firm and fixed principle of life, after the Bible doctrine of stewardship, tithes and offerings, and with the hope and prayer that this collection of Scriptures, stories, and prayers may make some contribution toward that end, this book is sent forth.

God is yearning for a chance to bless His people. He challenges them to give Him this chance. Like the young surgeon who stands fully equipped and thoroughly prepared awaiting only an opportunity. Like the young legal light who is abiding the day of his first great chance. When this opportunity is given, their fame breaks upon the world.

Even so, God awaits His opportunity which His people must provide. When they give it to Him, His fame and glory will break upon the world in a new and more wonderful way.

That opportunity will come when God's people bring their whole tithe into His storehouse — the Church.

Money is the least. Spiritual power is the larger. Unfaithfulness in handling that which is least (money) makes it impossible for God to bestow that which is larger (power). This explains the lack of spiritual power in many individuals and churches. Having been untrue in handling money, by robbing God of His part, God cannot trust them with the true riches, lest like Simon, the sorcerer (Acts 8:18), they use these also for selfish and personal ends. There is no need to pray until we pay. Spiritual blessing is conditioned upon material mastery. Prove to God that He can trust you by handling money aright, and then He will trust you with greater gifts.

The Prayer

Our Father, as we come this morning with our offerings of money — the currency of the world's markets — make us sensitive to the necessity of giving ourselves with our gifts, and thus offering our larger contribution to the world's need, through the ministry of personality. We thank Thee for the Divine currency of human personality — the currency of the Kingdom of God. This morning, make us to know the impotence of our gifts of money if unaccompanied by the larger gift of ourselves.

We humble ourselves, therefore, at Thy feet, and offer ourselves anew to Thy service. Multiply our offering this morning by the processes of Divine mathematics, and give to us, in the days and years ahead, the encouragement of seeing our personal investments magnified and multiplied in the lives of those with whom we come into contact. We thank Thee for the immortality of influence and the deathlessness of character, and pray Thee, this morning, that our gifts may be worthy of their immortal destiny. For Christ's sake. Amen.

Salvation: Past — Present — Future

We preach salvation because we believe that it is the greatest need. We do not preach sociology; we preach salvation. We do not preach economics; we preach evangelism. We do not preach culture; we preach conversion. We do not preach progress; we preach pardon. We do not preach a social order; we preach a new birth. We do not preach revolution; we preach regeneration. We do not preach restoration; we preach revival. We do not preach renunciation; we preach resurrection. We do not preach a new organization; we preach a new creation. We do not preach civilization; we preach Christ — Christ crucified for the salvation of men, who are dead in trespasses and in sin.

There must be a positive action in the acceptance of the new. The Gospel is the good news of God's grace in Christ by which He offers salvation to sinful men. To believe the Gospel is to believe in the *virgin-born*, the *virtuously living*, in the *vicariously dying*, in the *victoriously rising*, and the *visibly returning* Son of God. To believe the Gospel is to receive the riven, risen, reigning, returning Redeemer.

Christian joy is in doing good for others. Nehemiah said to the people: "This day is holy unto the Lord your God, mourn not, nor weep, but go your way, eat the fat, and drink the sweet, and send portions unto them for whom nothing is prepared, for this day is holy unto our Lord. Neither be ye sorry, for the joy of the Lord is your strength" (Neh. 8:9-10).

No joyful, victorious Christian is ever irritated when offered an opportunity to render service to others. He accepts the opportunity with joy, knowing that it is a testimony to the grace of God in Christ.

When Christians live in constant fellowship with God; when they see a continuous harvest of souls; when they drink water from the wells of salvation; when they have their prayers answered; when they live in the power of the Holy Spirit; when they keep God's commandments; when they do good to all men in the name of Christ; when they testify for Christ daily and hear others proclaiming Christ, then shall they indeed live joyful, victorious, triumphant, Christian lives. To such Christians Monday will be merciful and mirthful, Tuesday will be tearless, Wednesday will be wonderful, Thursday will be triumphant, and every Friday will be a good Friday, Saturday will be satisfying, and Sunday will be soulful indeed as the Lord's Day.

The heart of Dr. Dodd's ministry was winning the lost to Jesus and baptizing them. Here, in 1923, on a trip to the Holy Land, he baptizes E. A. Thorsell (left) in the Jordan River.

Salvation Neglected

Through the centuries, God has been using every possible means to get His message through to man, but so many things have caved in on man and covered him up making it difficult to reach him. We read stories of coal miners who have been closed in, deep down in the earth by caving walls. The stories tell of how desperately friends and loved ones on the surface work to get some word through to the entrapped men, and to get some word back as to whether they are still alive. We read stories of sunken submarines from which messages are sent and received by the process of tap, tap, tappings. God is constantly tapping out His messages to men. His last message is through Christ. If men do not receive that, He has nothing else to say to them. There are to be no more signs and symbols and riddles—no more thunderous tones of judgment in nature or from Sinai. God speaks now in the kindly cadences of sweet mercy and rich grace. There are to be no more messages in foreign tongues. God speaks now in the universal language of the heart. He speaks the language of love.

There are to be no more human priests for we now have Christ—a great High Priest who is better in every respect. He is better because He has entered into heaven itself. He is better than earthly priests because He is sympathetic and not cold. He is better because He is a Priest after

Melchisedec and not Aaron. He is better because He is a living, continuing Priest—never to die again. He died once and for all. He is better because He is a sinless High Priest. He is better because He made sacrifice once and for all, instead of daily as earthly priests do. He is a better High Priest because He is the substance of which others are only the shadow; because He is spiritual and not material; because He is eternal.

If you "neglect this so great salvation" in the great High Priest, there is no other hope. If you neglect this great salvation and fail to cultivate and develop it, by failing to study the Bible, to pray, to attend church services, and to work for Christ, then you may expect continued doubts and fears and anxieties, temptations and troubles.

Thank you, Lord, for saving my soul.
Thank you, Lord, for making me whole.
Thank you, Lord, for giving to me
Thy great salvation so rich and free.

RADIO REVIVAL SERMONS

The following sermons were broadcast over radio station KWKH in Shreveport, Louisiana, in 1932. Lest we forget—it was radio—coming from God's House. You heard things you could not see. Oh wonderful day when our minds were creative. But the greatest audience was Dr. Dodd's little mother in the countryside of Tennessee listening to her son over the radio with a trumpetlike loudspeaker to her ear.

Radio Station KWKH became so famous that when it was bought out and First Baptist Church went to another station, it was purchased by the Louisiana Hayride where Elvis Presley got his start.

A Revival of Faith

I have a deep conviction that the greatest need in these days of depression, anxiety, and uncertainty is "A Revival of Faith"—faith in God, faith in God's Word and work, faith in Christ and the Holy Spirit, faith in the church, faith in each other, and faith in ourselves.

And since "faith comes by hearing and hearing by the Word of God," I prayed for this opportunity to give God's Holy Word to the wings of the wind and to the ether of the night, that it might go forth with healing balm to all who would tune in.

Reports on these services came from as far east as Halifax, Nova Scotia, and as far west as Seattle, Washington, and San Bernardino, California. Reports came from every state in the Union, from all parts of Canada, Mexico, Central and South America, Cuba, Puerto Rico, and Panama.

Pastors reported that radios had been installed in their churches, colleges, hospitals, and homes had groups around their radios ranging in number from twenty-five to four hundred persons.

These sermons were chosen from sermons from my pulpit ministry and in special services throughout the country from Boston to Los Angeles and from Seattle to Miami. They are now sent forth in this form at the request of hundreds who heard them over the radio, and sent advance orders for them. It was these advance orders which made possible their publication.

These messages are now committed to the same blessed Spirit who has previously blessed them to the good of so many.

The Destroyer of Faith

S in originated with Satan. Sin is the worst enemy of the human family. Sin is its own best definition. I do not lay any claim to scholarship nor to the understanding of languages, but I have some acquaintance with the Hebrew of the Old Testament, with the Greek of the New Testament, with the Latin into which they were both first translated, and I have some knowledge of modern German, French, Italian, Spanish, and know something of our own language. And in each language with which I have any acquaintance the pronunciation of the word sin is its own best definition. There is something in it that carries its meaning in the very sound of the word. Take the word in our own language for example. Sin—s-i-n—sin! There is the hiss of the viper, the sting of the serpent, the poison of the asp, in the very pronunciation of the word. As we hear it hiss—s-s-sin!—there is the vigorous, vicious, venomous, vituperous viper of the dust as he slimes his wicked way across the pathway of man, lies in the sage grass and watches for every passerby that he may fasten his poisonous fangs into his body for destruction.

Christ's Memorial Supper

T hose who partake of the Lord's Supper are to turn their opened eyes of faith back to the Cross, are to lift up their opened eyes of hope to

Christ's coming again, and are to open their hearts of love to fellowship with his Spirit.

The Lord's Supper deals with believers in three tenses—past, present, and future. As to the past, it is a commemoration. As to the present, it is a meditation. As to the future, it is an anticipation.

This expression "till He come" was the password among the early Christians. When they met one another in the crowded streets of the city, in dark places at night, or elsewhere, their word of greeting and recognition was, "Till He come."

The pagan rulers, officers of the law, and people were so bitter in their persecutions of the Christians that it was necessary for the Christians to maintain much secrecy. One can easily imagine how the face of a Christian would light up as he met someone whom he did not know and from whom he might fear bodily injury, when that one would give the password, "Till He come." This password would insure kindness, consideration, and fellowship.

But this password would do even more. It would fan the flame of hope and joyful anticipation of the world to come in the hearts of those who were being persecuted and tried in this world. It would stimulate strength, create courage, and brighten hope for carrying on "till He come."

This is one of the sublime objects of the Lord's Supper. The Lord's Supper is intended to fix the eyes of the disciples on that coming event of such glorious significance.

The Lord's Supper is a beautiful memorial—yes, we shall never cease to observe it as such. But it is also a prophecy.

The Lord's Supper looks both ways, backward and forward, and binds the past and the future together.

We have multiplied our messages upon the Supper as a memorial and minimized them upon the subject of His coming again. Who of us has ever heard of a communion service or meditation being held with a definite mission and message of foretelling Christ's coming? D. L. Moody one time remarked that, in all the observances of the Lord's Supper in which he had engaged in various cities of the world, he had never heard it mentioned as related to Christ's coming.

The Lord's Supper is intended to "nourish gratitude and stimulate hope." There is nothing that can do this like the fixing of the eyes upon Christ's coming again.

"Till He come."

How that expression rings and sings, how it glows and gleams, how it thrills and throbs, how it stirs and stimulates!

"Till He come." This creates courage and gives hope to carry on.

"Till He come" is a beacon star by which men safely steer their course in days when there are confusion and bewilderment, in days of uncertainty, anxiety, depression, and distress.

His coming will make all things right.

This is the meaning of the Lord's Supper; and those who fail to participate in the Lord's Supper miss this strengthening message. Those who fail to observe the Lord's Supper as a prophecy and a promise of His coming likewise miss much of its blessing.

Christians who regularly attend the Lord's Supper grow gradually stronger, better, happier, and more useful.

Christians who habitually neglect attendance upon the Lord's Supper grow colder, harder, and more useless.

"Let a man examine himself, and so let him eat."

Missions Our Mission

The object of this book is twofold: First, to show that our entire denominational Cooperative Program (orphans' homes, hospitals, ministerial relief, Christian education, city missions, state missions, home missions, and foreign missions) is ONE. It is not to be looked upon in segments with each worker over in a corner attending to his own little job entirely apart from the others. They are all in the same room working at the same table with the same common end in view. Much less are they antagonistic to each other. They are not competitors but cooperators in a common cause. What helps one helps all. What hurts one hurts all. They must all stand or fall together. To seek to put one of these departments over against the other is detrimental to all.

The second object of this book is to show that the ultimate aim and end of all the work, whether it be the support of chanceless children, the healing in our hospitals of humanity's hurt, the taking care of aged and worn-out ministers and missionaries, the support of Christian educational institutions, the employment of evangelists, teachers, editors, mission secretaries, and missionaries, the aim of it all is the preaching of the gospel to every creature.

Missions — The Mission of Our Healing Ministry

Christianity is the one religion that exalts the human body. Heathen religions abuse and debase the body. Paganism developed a certain form of physical prowess, but it had no conception of the real sanctity of the body.

The Christian view of the human body is that it is sacred and should be kept clean, wholesome, and healthy (1 Cor. 6:13-20).

The body is the creative work of God. The first man, Adam, was the crowning glory of God's creation, stamped with the divine image, made holy and healthy, and made to live forever. But Adam brought disease and death to his body by sin.

The second man, Jesus Christ, was also holy and healthy. He never sinned. He was never sick. He should not have died but for our sins. Death came to His body only because He bore the sins of others.

The human body, having been brought under the power of death by sin, becomes the object of Christ's redeeming mercy: "Ye are not your own; ye are bought with a price" (1 Cor. 6:20).

The body, which has been redeemed by the grace of God in Christ, is the temple of the Holy Spirit (1 Cor. 6:19).

Missions — The Mission of Money Raising

Getting money for oneself is good business. Getting money for God is a great art. Money within itself is nothing. What money represents is everything. As wages, it represents service rendered. As profits, it represents business achievements. *As gifts, it represents coined character and Christian consecration.*

Three Sixteens

In our search for the oil fields of God's grace we have decided to establish a location in the third chapter of Matthew at verse sixteen.

Matthew 3:16

"And when Jesus was baptized, he went up immediately from the water and behold, the heavens were opened and he saw the Spirit of God descending like a dove, and alighting on him; . . ."

You cannot conceive of a person here in a body without a brain or heart. You can conceive of a person as a spirit without a brain or a body. Oh, yes you can, because some of you tell me, "I'll be with you at church in spirit, but I have to go see Grandma next Sunday." I have been preaching to spirits sitting in empty pews a long time and have never had a convert among them yet. I had rather see the body and brain along with the spirit. It takes the three to make a whole person.

1 Corinthians 3:16

"Do you know that you are God's temple and that God's Spirit dwells in you?"

Acts 3:16

"And his name, by faith in his name, has made this man strong whom you see and know; and the faith which is through Jesus has given the man this perfect health in the presence of you all."

Ephesians 3:16

". . . that according to the riches of his glory he may grant you to be strengthened with might through his Spirit in the inner man, . . ."

2 Timothy 3:16

"All scripture is inspired by God and profitable for teaching, for reproof, for correction, and for training in righteousness, . . ."

Intelligent people, rational people, sensible people ought to understand that it is more reasonable to believe in a Trinity than to believe in Unitarianism. The three are necessary to make up the one person.

2 Peter 3:16

"There are some things in them [Paul's letters] hard to understand, which the ignorant and unstable twist to their own destruction, as they do the other scriptures."

So it is in the God-head—God the Father is the intelligent nature of Deity, God the Son is the physical manifestation of Deity, and God the Holy Ghost is the spiritual revelation of Deity. These three manifestations or revelations, or projections of Deity into the conscious life of man compose the whole, the complete God.

Colossians 3:16

"Let the word of Christ dwell in you richly, teach and admonish one another in all wisdom, and sing psalms and hymns and spiritual songs with thankfulness in your hearts to God."

The greatest one of all the 3:16s of the Bible is John 3:16. I ask you to come with me, this morning, for a meditation on John 3:16.

John 3:16

"For God so loved the world that he gave his only Son, that whoever believes in him should not perish but have eternal life."

Every word of that verse shines like a star and glitters like a gem. "God," the omnipotent, the eternal, the infinite, the omniscient, the omnipresent, God.

∞

For God so loved the world,
He gave His only Son,
To die on Calv'ry's tree,
From sin to set me free.
Some day He's coming back
What glory that will be.
Wonderful His love to me.

Jesus Is Coming To Earth Again

The theme of the whole Bible gathers around Christ, the central personage of all the centuries. Christianity is Christ, the living Son of God who was dead and is alive forever more.

And this theme is in three parts, He Is Coming, He Has Come, and He Is Coming Again.

If the Old Testament announcement that He is coming was important, and if the people of God were in those days justified in meditating much upon that theme; and if the announcement in the Gospels that He has come was important to the New Testament saints, how much more important to the saints of today is the final announcement He is coming again!

It is the design, therefore, of this book, and the sincerest hope and prayer of the author, that the pages here written may be blessed of our heavenly Father in strengthening the faith and brightening the hope of all God's children under whose eyes it may fall.

The Second Coming of Christ is a glorious doctrine. Paul calls it "That blessed hope." It is an inspiring, encouraging, and gloom-dispelling doctrine.

By the Second Coming of Christ we mean the personal, visible, audible, bodily appearance of our Lord Jesus Christ upon this earth again.

That the footprints of God may be seen in the histories of nations and in the history of the world is clear to every thinking man. But these manifestations of divine power and sovereign oversight of human affairs do not mean the Second Coming of Christ.

That the hand of God may be seen in great providential manifestations is certainly true. Earthquakes are sometimes the tread of His feet, storms and tornadoes the breath of His mouth, and clouds but the dust from His chariot wheels. But this is not what we mean by the Second Coming of Christ.

That it has been given to many of the saints of God to see the face of the living Saviour and to feel the touch of His hand upon theirs in the hour and article of death, is as certain as the promises of Christ are true. But this is not what we mean by the Second Coming of Christ.

The Second Coming of Christ means the personal, visible, audible, bodily appearance of the Lord Jesus Christ on this earth again.

That there are three hundred and eighteen references in the New Testament alone to the Second Coming of Christ is a fact which at once exalts the doctrine into a prominence that cannot be avoided. If God considers the doctrine of sufficient importance to give one out of every thirty-five New Testament verses to it, who are we that we should evade it with a wave of the hand? This is not saying that a doctrine is to be valued merely by the number of references which it has in the Scriptures. If God should say a thing only once, it would be sufficiently important to demand our most careful consideration. But since He sees fit to speak so often of Jesus' Second Coming, it is certainly clear that He desires to impress it indelibly upon our minds by the process of line upon line and precept upon precept.

This is the one place in the Bible where we are told to comfort one another with certain words. And the words which we are given refer to the coming again of our Lord Jesus to this earth. It is the one inspiring hope which heals the broken heart, gives peace to the heaving bosom, brushes away the tears of the disconsolate, and gilds the grave with glory.

You can hear the lift of the chorus as the young people sing . . .

> Some day He's coming
> O wondrous, blessed day
> O yes, all because of Calvary.

The Living Christ

Dr. Dodd was the first Baptist Hour speaker — here are some gleanings from that first sermon:

H as he not said, "In all thy ways acknowledge him, and he shall direct thy paths"?

And, amid all these crises, Paul lifted up the Christ and said, "Here is your answer to every problem." Christ has always stood out more prominently,

Dr. Dodd at the pulpit.

shone forth more gloriously, and towered more triumphantly in the midst of crises. A crisis is a challenge to strength. Weakness quails and fails in crises. This is why Paul could present Christ as the answer to human need. Paul could say of Christ, "He is not weak, but to you is mighty," while for himself and for all who would accept Christ as Saviour and Lord, he could say, "Thanks be to God, who giveth us the victory through our Lord Jesus Christ."

In every crisis of human history, Christ has met the challenge. The crisis through which the world is presently passing is another challenge to Christ and to Christians. It will be met as in past ages, with courage, consecration, and conviction.

Has he not said: "In all thy ways acknowledge him, and he shall direct thy paths"? There is the old story of the futility by which the Continental Congress had been working. Then, the aged Benjamin Franklin arose to say: "Mr. President, I am convinced that we cannot reach agreements without that wisdom which comes from above. I have long observed the affairs of men in this regard. I suggest that we pause for prayer." It was done. Guidance was given. The United States of America was born. Yes, God, as revealed in the grace and glory of his Son, Jesus Christ, can settle all human affairs, if only men will submit them to Him.

The world's welter of wickedness at this moment; the wars, and rumors of wars, their roaring airplanes and belching big berthas hurling their missiles of death and damnation upon helpless women and children, are all the result of man having forsaken God. The feverish futility under which other nations are working will come to naught, and in the same manner, our nation, too, unless we confess our personal sins, our national iniquities, and call upon him, who is mighty to save and to lead us out of the mess into which ambitious, greedy, and selfish men have led the world. It is either Christ or chaos, religion or revolution, redemption or rejection. We in America still have it within our power to decide which it shall be.

He lives, He lives, Christ Jesus lives today!
He walks with me and talks with me along life's narrow way.
He lives, He lives, salvation to impart.
You ask me how I know He lives?
He lives within my heart.

THANK YOU, SUNDAY SCHOOL BOARD OF THE SOUTHERN Baptist Convention in Nashville, Tennessee for publishing the following book in 1923. It has been the hardest to make into half notes.

The Prayer Life of Jesus
Foreword

Prayer is a most engaging subject. The possibilities of prayer are beyond enumeration. We are encouraged to pray for our temporal needs. "Give us this day our daily bread" is a temporal as well as a heart cry. "Our Father" is the longing for companionship and paternal comradeship. The hunger of the soul is satisfied. Eternal praise is on our lips; humbleness of spirit is wrought within us; boldness of approach is encouraged; ideals are inspired; and walking with God is cultivated by prayer. It is the one universal appeal which our Father never denies.

What Jesus said about prayer and how He encouraged His followers to pray, have been the theme of His people in all ages. This theme has cultivated the atmosphere of prayerfulness. Historians have lingered to record His words; exegetes have expounded His teaching; human experiences have attested His meaning; and here poets have raised their loftiest hymns.

But our Brother Dodd has, with great spiritual intuition, emphasized a phase of our Lord's prayer life which has generally been overlooked. Others have told how our Lord prayed and what He said about prayer. Dr. Dodd enters the Holy of Holies and brings to our understanding how prayer reacted upon the Lord Himself. These hours when Jesus prayed, whether in the lonely mountain or in Gethsemane, touch the most intimate scenes of His earthly life. No other book touches this phase of the prayer life of Jesus.

It was with thrilling delight that hundreds heard Dr. Dodd lecture on these themes. His coming to the Baptist Bible Institute (New Orleans Baptist Theological Seminary) to lecture on this subject was keenly anticipated. His gracious and spiritual words met every expectation and not only satisfied his numerous hearers but likewise marked a distinct high place in the most exalted month the Baptist Bible Institute has ever known.

This book is sent forth in its mission of love with the expressed hope that it will quicken others and lead to more devout communion with the Father as the Spoken Message did for those of us who were fortunate enough to hear these lectures.

John T. Christian
Baptist Bible Institute
New Orleans, La.

Preface

This series of studies is the substance of addresses which have been given to various Young People's assemblies, Bible Conferences, and General Assemblies throughout the country.

It is not intended to cover all the subject of prayer; not even all the phases of prayer that Jesus Himself touched. Neither the Model Prayer which He gave His disciples in the sixth chapter of Matthew's Gospel, and which has been the subject of many volumes, nor anything else that He said about prayer, is touched.

It has been my purpose to discover what Jesus did, what He said, and what happened in His own personal private and public prayers.

It appears to me that the greatest need of the Kingdom of God and of the world today is more intercessors, more of God's remembrances who give Him no rest day or night. But the need is just as great that those who pray shall know how to pray. There is too much prayerless praying.

If this little look into the prayer life of our Lord shall help anywhere in increasing the number of those who pray, and increasing the power of those who have been praying by virtue of their following the example of Jesus, then I shall be abundantly repaid for this humble effort.

M. E. Dodd
Pastor's Study
First Baptist Church
Shreveport, La.

The Prayer Life of Jesus

No man ever accomplished so many tasks in so brief a span of time as did Jesus. And yet no man ever spent more time in prayer than did He. Perhaps it would be better to say it this way: No man ever accomplished more than did Jesus because no man ever devoted as much time to prayer.

Prayer, to Jesus, meant fellowship with the Great Father. Prayer was the means of "getting things from God." Prayer was the refuge from life's storms. Prayer planned the Kingdom movements, selected the apostles, established the church. Prayer warded off the fiery darts of the enemy until the fullness of time for their final fury to burst on Him, and then prayer prepared the Lord for the worst. Prayer was His safety valve which released the pent-up passions and gave vent to the smoldering fires within.

Jesus began His public ministry with a prayer at the holy ordinance of His baptism (Luke 3:12) and closed it with a petition in the midst of the agonies of the cross. Prayer to Him was both an act and atmosphere. In it He lived, moved, and had His being. He met every emergency, faced every difficulty, conquered every foe by the power of prayer.

There is no force within the reach of man so vitally necessary to meet the impending dangers of the day as that of believing prayer. And there is no one who can teach us to pray as does our Lord. We shall, therefore, walk with Him through the Gospels from His baptism to Calvary, observing His ways and words, His conduct and character, His place and posture, His meaning and accomplishment while at prayer.

The source of our information for this study is, of course, the four Gospels; or rather the Gospel as revealed by the four writers, Matthew, Mark, Luke, and John. The composite picture of the four gives us the perfect Christ, and we are to look for the perfect Christ at His highest exercise as seen in the act of prayer. "Praying is the very highest energy of which the human soul is capable."

The masterpieces of art are reproduced in all their beautifully blending colors by a process of photography and printing which gives to us in prints a magnificent and perfect reproduction of the original.

The photographic instrument is so arranged with certain colored glass and lenses that when placed before the painting it allows only certain rays of light to penetrate, for example, the purple. From that film a photograph is made, then a half-tone cut, and from this the first impression of the painting is produced. Once more the camera is changed by transfer of the colored glass so that other certain rays of light are permitted to penetrate, for example, the blue. From this the cut is made and thus the second impression is printed over the previous piece. This process continues through just as many times as there are different colors to be reproduced. When the last impression is made, we have a perfect reproduction of the painting.

This is the process followed by the writers of the Gospel in their work of reproducing the Masterpiece of all time, the Lord Jesus Christ. Matthew turned his camera upon that matchless Man and drew forth the royal rays of His Kingship and stamped that in his part of the Gospel. Mark came with his camera and drew out the blue rays of loyal service as Jehovah's servant and stamped that on the print. Luke drew forth the pure life of a perfect Manhood and made this impression with his Gospel. John's instrument penetrated the Eternities and photographed the Christ who was and is and is to be, the Pre-existent, Eternal Son of God, and stamped that upon the print.

And these four give us the perfect picture of the perfect Man and of the perfect God.

To me personally there are certain places where, when praying, heaven comes a bit nearer and the Lord seems a bit dearer.

One of these is a country roadside in Tennessee, along which I trudged, a barefoot thirteen-year-old boy, for many weary nights to the little country church house during the revival meetings in search of salvation.

Twenty-five years afterward when I had gone through school and college and had become pastor of a great city church I was invited back there to hold a meeting in the same little country church. At the close of the first service, the pastor said: "We are going to Brother Butler's for dinner—have you any preference as to the road we shall take." I expressed the desire to go along a certain way, and arriving at a certain spot I asked him to stop while I should find as nearly as possible the place of the great experience of a quarter of a century ago when such a great change had been wrought in my heart. Finding the very tree by the side of which on that wonderful night I had knelt in prayer, I knelt down once again. A flood of memories swept through my soul. I remembered the burden I had felt for sin, the terrible consciousness of guilt before God. I remembered how in desperation I had sought peace a thousand ways to find; and how at last on that wonderful night I had stopped on this roadside to commit myself to Christ. There I had lifted up my despairing cry for mercy; and there had seen the tenderness and compassion of that sweetest of all faces; and there had heard the sweetest words that ever fell on mortal ears, the words—"Thy sins be forgiven thee." There I had found the peace of God that passeth all understanding, that peace which the world can never give nor take away. It was a holy place; it was a sacred place. And now, twenty-five years afterward, it was a Bethel to my heart. Prayer seemed more real. God seemed nearer because of this sacred place, my shrine of prayer.

When I started overseas with our soldiers, I passed again through Tennessee and Kentucky to say "good-bye" to my friends. I visited the town of my first pastorate after leaving college. After a public service and a few personal calls on some real old friends I asked that I might go to the little village cemetery. I did not know how a journey over the seas in the midst of war's desolation and destruction would end. I needed more of the assurance of Divine power and help. I did not know where I could find it so quickly as on one sacred little spot of earth out in that cemetery. So I went there. Some kind friends had anticipated the visit and had carried fragrant flowers to the little grave. Arriving there, the other friends, with keen spiritual perception, knowing that I desired to be left alone, passed on. There alone in the quiet place "I met the Master face to face."

Kneeling beside the little grave under the sobbing cedars, memories of that Christmas time, a dozen years before, returned. There with the falling snows we had put the little one in the cold earth. There came also memories of God's glorious hand and marvelous grace which in infinite love came upon me that sad time. And prayer at this sacred place was made more real. Call it mere sentiment if you will; sentiment is the thing that brings God close to us. Man by the road of reason alone cannot find God.

Prayer has a tremendously transforming power. If it has become a fixed habit of life, the glory of it will work out into the face and features, character and conduct. The prayer life of Jesus, which was a great part of His whole life, reached one of its greatest climaxes in the transfiguration. It was while He was praying that the "fashion of his countenance was altered."

This glory of God that shone in the face of Jesus Christ was not a pantomime. It was not the shining of a light from the outside, but the shining forth of that which was on the inside. It was not a tacked-on glory, but an out-working splendor.

Here is a great illustration of the reflex influence of prayer. Jesus had fed His mind and heart and life upon fellowship with the Father and upon spiritual food until they now reveal themselves in His person.

This is as tragically true of things that are bad as of things that are good. One becomes like the things he feeds upon. Down in Central Park, New York, I was watching the beasts and the birds at feeding time. There were two birds side by side in separate cages which made a great impression upon me. One of them was the vulture. He was feeding upon the filth of carrion. His feathers were ragged, dirty, and filthy. His head was crusty and rusty and repulsive. His feet and beak were filthy with the food upon which he was feasting. I turned away from it with revulsion. In the other cage was a bird of paradise. He was delicately picking out of the finely winnowed grain only the soundest seeds. He was extraordinarily careful of his food. His body was beautiful. His face was delightfully pleasing to look upon. His feathers were as delicate as the finest maidenhair fern. The fine food upon which he had fed all of his life had worked itself out into his personal appearance. The contrast between the two birds was startling. It is a great law of nature and grace that one becomes like that upon which he feeds.

Herein is the great value of private or family Bible reading and prayers just before retiring at night. Psychology teaches us that the subconscious mind never sleeps. It is really more active when we are asleep than when we are awake. It certainly is more influential in the production of character during our sleeping hours than our wakeful ones because when we are awake it is consumed with outside activities. Many of us can recall the experience of having solved some mathematical problem while asleep, over which we had pondered many wakeful hours with poor success.

If one goes to bed with the beautiful thoughts of the Bible in his mind and with the conscious presence of God in his soul after prayer, he is bound to experience in life the glorious outworking of such powers. This is why the old-time family altar, with Bible reading and prayers before retiring, such as is so beautifully described in Burns's "The Cotter's Saturday Night" was such a tremendous force in the production of great men and women.

People will say, "I do not seem to have a straight line to heaven." But, God has an 800 number: 1—800—PRAYER. The prayer of Jesus takes another great step forward and says, "Thou hearest me always." He could say, "Thou hearest me always," because in His prayer life there were none of those hindrances to prayer which are specified in the Scriptures as the explanation for so much of our own unanswered prayer.

Selfishness is the first and greatest hindrance. "Ye ask, and receive not, because ye ask amiss, that ye may spend it in your own pleasures" (James 4:3).

Sin is a great hindrance to prayer. "Behold, the Lord's hand is not shortened, that it cannot save; neither his ear heavy, that it cannot hear. But your iniquities have separated between you and your God, and your sins have hid his face from you, that he will not hear" (Isa. 59:1–2).

Iniquity in the heart stands in the way of many a prayer. "If I regard iniquity in my heart, the Lord will not hear me" (Ps. 66:18).

Idol worshippers need not expect to receive anything of God. "Son of man, these men have set up their idols in their heart, and put the stumbling block of their iniquity before their face: should I be enquired of at all by them?" (Ezek. 14:3). An idol worshipper is one who puts somebody else first and God second.

Enmity in the heart will block the path of prayer. "And when ye stand praying, forgive, if he have ought against any: that your Father also which is in heaven may forgive you your trespasses" (Mark 11:25).

Bitterness and unkindness in social relationships are barriers to prayer. "Likewise, ye husbands, dwell with them according to knowledge, giving honor unto the wife as unto the weaker vessel, and as being heirs together of the grace of life; that your prayers be not hindered" (1 Pet. 3:7).

Refusing to hear and respond to the cry of the poor will stop the ears of God to our cry. "Whoso stoppeth his ears at the cry of the poor, he also shall cry himself, but shall not be heard" (Prov. 21:13).

But Jesus had neither selfishness nor sin, nor iniquity nor idols, nor enmity nor unkindness, nor lack of charity in His heart or life. Therefore, He could say, "Thou hearest me always."

All prayer must begin with a prayer for ourselves—Psalm 51:10.

Those Bible characteristics of prevailing prayer were always present in the prayer life of our Lord.

He could pray always according to God's will. "And this is the confidence that we have in Him, that, if we ask any thing according to His will, He heareth us" (1 John 5:14).

His prayers were unceasingly persistent. "And He spake a parable unto them to this end, that men ought always to pray and not to faint" (Luke 18:1).

His prayers were in deepest truth and sincerity. "The Lord is nigh unto all them that call upon Him, to all that call upon Him in truth" (Ps. 145:18).

His life was beautifully obedient to the law of God. "And whatsoever we ask, we receive of Him, because we keep His commandments, and do those things that are pleasing in His sight" (1 John 3:22).

Therefore, because He prayed conformably, persistently, sincerely, and obediently, He could say, "Thou hearest me always." His was the prayer of the righteous man which availeth much in its working (James 5:16).

"Thou hast heard me;" "Thou hearest me always." What wonderful words! How much more wonderful that they are true! Oh, to be able to pray as Jesus prayed! always to be heard, and always to be answered.

But some of our prayers are so selfish and so foolish and so contradictory that they cannot be answered. God cannot answer both parties when two persons are praying for exactly opposite things. He may not answer either. But He will answer the one who prays according to His will, for the best.

In this way we may pray as Jesus did and then be able to say, "Always Thou hearest me." God does hear and answer every real prayer.

What glorious inspiration is this intercessory prayer of Christ for us! It is good to know that there are friends and loved ones constantly bearing us up in their prayers before the Father. To have a band of personal intercessors throughout the country is a joy and unspeakable glory.

I stepped into my prayer meeting room one night when my people thought I was out of the city and as I entered, they were in prayer. One of the deacons was saying, "God, bless our pastor; clothe him always with power in his work; give him Thy grace and wisdom for his tasks; encourage his heart by prospering the work of the Lord in his hands."

That prayer gave my heart a great thrill. It was not said for my ears because he did not know I was present, but it was said to the Father. To have a praying wife and praying children is a great blessing. To have a praying father and mother is the very acme of earth's crown. To know that at a certain hour each evening a gray-haired mother from her invalid chair is pouring forth a torrent of petitions in behalf of the faraway son is inspiration and encouragement inexpressible.

But beyond all of these and above and better than any of them is the inspiring thought that while the Lord of Glory was here on this earth, He spanned the centuries with His piercing eye and caught a glimpse of me, and understanding my weaknesses and my needs, lifted up His voice in earnest petition and prayed that, ultimately, I might be with Him where He is.

Glorious prayer!

"Lord, teach us to pray."

ON THE WINGS OF AN ANGEL THE NOTES OF A SONG FLOAT by and inhabit my heart and soul—can you hear the strains of music?

> Whisper a prayer in the morning,
> Whisper a prayer at noon.
> Whisper a prayer in the evening
> To keep your heart in tune.
>
> God answers prayer in the morning,
> God answers prayer at noon.
> God answers prayer in the evening,
> If your heart is kept in tune.

These choruses were sung at church, assemblies, and during wars all across our nation. They spread the word because they warmed our hearts. We love the lift of our sacred classical music, but every music graduate knows that along with the tenderloin—the best cut of the beef—we need a piece of bread.

Thank you, B. B. McKenney, for all the hymns you have written that still grace our Baptist Hymnals. Thank you for the encouragement in our prayer lives because—

> Jesus may come in the morning,
> Jesus may come at noon;
> Jesus may come in the evening,
> So, keep your heart in tune.

Half notes have come to a rest and so must I. My hand will be stayed and refreshment must come with a breathing space.

I had gone to bed and at 1:30 A.M., the Lord awakened me—calling me by name like He did little Samuel. If this has happened to you—identify, if not, silent be.

"Get up," He said. "Half notes is not finished. It needs to be held a little longer and made whole."

"Tell me how, Lord." He did and then said, "Get up and write it down."

"I will remember and do it in the morning."

"No, you will forget—do it now."

I lay there and finally just before 2:00 A.M., I went to my desk.

"This chapter is Dr. Dodd's life," the Lord said. "His books are telling us what he did best—a preacher—a deliverer of the message of the Lord Jesus Christ."

Still half asleep, I said, "Lord, I really don't understand completely—a whole note is equal in value to four quarter notes or two half notes."

Did I hear a sigh from above? Yes, but patience came and He said no more except, "Listen to the music."

My mind was so fixed as to what the whole note meant on earth

In 1951, Dr. Dodd participated in a Shreveport crusade with the Reverend Billy Graham (left).

that I did not see the eternal beat that never stops. Then, as I was sitting there in the middle of the night, the Scripture came to me. "Be still and know that I am God. . . ."

I was still. Finally, I heard the music that I had heard all my life; but now, it showed me the whole note. "Thank you, Lord for saving my soul; Thank you, Lord for making me whole."

Then came . . . "His love is in my heart, Never to depart. His blood has made me whole."

Then from the "Sketch of M. E. Dodd". . . . If I can make the sour notes whole and beautiful again. . . . "Lord, I see what you mean. These half notes are the whole note—the whole note on the spiritual scale of life."

Dr. Dodd preached that whole note to the limit. He drove his heart preaching the gospel. "Don't go to California," came from everyone. He just smiled and said, "I am as close to heaven in California as in Shreveport." And so he was.

His heart never stopped beating. The last heartbeat on earth was the first heartbeat in heaven. "Go ye into all the world."

And he went. Only you reading these words can hold that note—go ring the bells that Jesus Christ was born. When you accept Christ as your personal Lord and Saviour, He makes you whole!

Perfect Ten

AS DUSK DREW NIGH, THE STILLNESS OF THE EVENING WAS broken at the Dodd home by the ringing of the telephone. It was not of a musical sound and rings can disturb, but sometimes it is God Himself Who dials the number. There is no doubt that the ten rules for living and for worship that God revealed to Moses on Mount Sinai were going to climb a mountaintop again for God's people.

The editor of the *Shreveport Times* — the leading newspaper — was calling to speak to Dr. Dodd who was now retired.

"Of all your famous sermons you have preached through the years, I would like to put the one you think was your very best in the newspaper."

A long pause and Dr. Dodd said, "You will put in the paper whatever sermon I send?"

"That we will," the editor answered.

Dr. Dodd sent the 10 Commandments and they published it in a 1952 edition of the *Shreveport Times*.

The *Shreveport Times* continues to flow with the Perfect Ten.

COPY OF TEN COMMANDMENTS IS SENT TO GOVERNMENT LEADERS

Accompanied by an inspiring letter signed by Dr. M. E. Dodd, pastor emeritus, the First Baptist Church of Shreveport has sent to all government officials in Baton Rouge and Washington a copy of the Ten Commandments as a standard of ethics for all, with the hope and the prayer that they may be strengthened in their moral purpose.

The copy is in blue on white paper with red border, representing the national colors. It is attractive and on display in offices of the officials, will direct attention to an unsurpassable sermon.

This religious gesture offers great possibilities. It reflects growing recognition of the need of more moral influences in connection with public affairs as well as in connection with all other affairs having to do with the welfare of the people, individually and as collective groups.

In the letter bearing Dr. Dodd's signature, the government officials are given this solemn message, which every religious-minded person should always respect with efforts to influence others:

> For some time there has been a lot of discussion about a code of ethics for government officials and employees.
>
> We present herewith a very old code in a form which we trust will be attractive enough to warrant its display in a prominent place in your office or chambers.
>
> This document you will readily recognize as the decalogue and the expression of God's wisdom and will for man in man's relationship, first: to God (I-II-III-IV) and second: to his fellow man (V-X).
>
> You are aware also that these commandments have been the foundation of all civilized nations for three thousand years. From them stem all just and righteous laws.
>
> Furthermore, the enlightened conscience of the world's foremost religions, Jewish, Protestant, and Catholic, give hearty assent to the proposition that all who keep them, will be blessed and all who violate them suffer loss.

To display this code of ethics in the government offices and chambers is suggested by the Shreveport church through its pastor emeritus, who for decades served the congregation here actively and preached and rendered other religious services in many lands.

Perfect means without defect—faultless—pure—absolute—infinite—divine—rare—matchless—moral—true—untarnished—brightest jewel in the crown. You did very well, Mr. Dictionary!

But should these Perfect Ten still stretch across our land? A thousand times—Yes! Did you know we have people in the U. S. of A. that worship

A Standard of Ethics for All

I Am Jehovah Thy God

I
Thou shalt have no other gods before me.

II
Thou shalt not make unto thee any graven image.

III
Thou shalt not take the name of the Lord thy God in vain.

IV
Remember the Sabbath Day to keep It holy.

V
Honor thy Father and thy Mother.

VI
Thou shalt not kill.

VII
Thou shalt not commit adultery.

VIII
Thou shalt not steal.

IX
Thou shalt not bear false witness.

X
Thou shalt not covet.

Exodus 20:2-17

First Baptist Church
Shreveport, La.

When the Shreveport Times agreed to publish one of Dr. Dodd's sermons, he sent them this copy of the Ten Commandments.

their own god and we would not want to offend them?

Father, forgive us for being so generous in freedom of worship that we put our standard bearer in the dust. Let them worship their foreign gods, but not take away our In God We Trust and We pledge allegiance under God. People's footprints found their way to America, not to worship another god — just in their own way. It was and always will be just one God.

CHAPTER 13

The Chimes
Strike Twelve

TEN O'CLOCK PACIFIC COAST TIME—"DR. DODD, WORLD-Famed Minister Dies Of A Heart Attack"—rang the news out over the air, but in a certain city, the chimes struck twelve!

Yes, it was midnight in Shreveport, the end of the day. The newspaper came, and it was like the unfolding of a scroll. The headlines seemed darker than usual; as if they had been drenched with ink. The huge black letters of the headline were towering and heartbreaking, closing in with finality—"Dr. Dodd Dies in California." Then the article continued.

Heart Attack is Fatal—Wife at Bedside When End Comes in Hospital. Died suddenly late Wednesday night in Long Beach, California, August 6, 1952—Dodd was 73. Supplying at First Baptist Church, Glendale, for two summer months, the well-known Baptist leader had been in extremely ill health since he was stricken with a heart attack while conducting an evangelistic meeting in Panama City, Florida, some three years ago.

WORLD LEADER—CITY MOURNS

"People throughout the world will mourn the passing of Dr. M.E. Dodd," said Shreveport's Mayor Clyde E. Fant.

"He was blessed with the unusual talent and ability of a great leader . . . and he helped move a whole world closer to God," one admirer said.

"Here in Shreveport, we have lost a great spiritual and civic leader. While in body, Dr. Dodd has left us, his great influence for good will live on for generations to come," said Monsignor Plauche, pastor of Holy Trinity Catholic Church and dean of the Catholic clergy in the city.

Another admirer commented, "We have lost a friend from the Roundtable of the National Conference of Christians and Jews."

"His passing is a great loss . . ." on and on the columns read, and in the papers that followed, expressions were manifested from all corners of the earth—yes, they remembered when he girdled the globe for God.

But wait! There is an echo coming back. Yes, listen! It's coming from the Huntington Hotel in Long Beach, California, just a few hours before the chimes struck twelve.

"Emma, I am going to the office to find the young preacher who is to take us to our engagement tonight."

"Hurry back, Sweetheart."

"I will. I won't be gone long."

But it was long . . . much too long. Oh, those minutes that tick can seem like an eternity . . . especially when our heart knows the inevitable. Have you ever tried to keep a thoroughbred race horse still? You can hold the reins, but you can still feel the tug for the open path and the race. All during M. E. Dodd's life, people had tried to hold the reins for his own good. But, his was a race against time . . . winning people to the Lord . . . "for ye know neither the day nor the hour wherein the son of man cometh."

His exhortation to ministers and lay Christians alike, "Save yourself and others you cannot save," had fallen from his lips so many times based on the Scripture passage found in Acts 20:23–24.

He went to the office but the one he sought was not there. Coming out again into the open, he stood in awe of the majestic beauty about him—yes, God's fashion show.

"Lord, why can't I find that young man who is supposed to go with us tonight? I need him to take me where I am going."

"Now, M. E.," said the Lord, "Are you sure you need that young man to take you where you are going?"

"The time is fleeing so swiftly," Dr. Dodd thought to himself, "I had better get back to Emma. I don't want her to be uneasy."

As he made his way back to the hotel, his eye caught sight of a television that was displayed in a store window; he paused to watch it a few minutes— television had not come to Shreveport as yet—they were waiting.

Time goes into oblivion when your thoughts are absorbed until something strikes a chord within and you lower your eyes to your watch.

"My, it's getting late. I have been out longer than I realized. I must get back to Emma. She will be worrying."

As he walked back, he couldn't help but think of the goodness of God. How marvelous that He had permitted them to be together through such a long journey of faith.

"Bless her heart. What would I have done without her all these wonderful years?" Lofty thoughts were interrupted by a euphony of heavenly music.

"That music . . . where is it coming from? It sounds a little like the chimes in Shreveport . . . only I believe that quality is more beautiful. I am glad no one can hear me . . . for I wouldn't admit that to anyone but myself."

"Young man, could you tell me where that exquisite music is coming from? Is it from a building or is it from a church nearby?"

"I do not hear any music, Sir."

"You mean you don't hear that music?"

"No, Sir."

"Well, thank you, Son."

"I must be mistaken. No one else heard those crystalline tones. I must be homesick, or maybe thinking of Emma made everything seem alive with music."

Back in the hotel, Emma was listening with an anxious heart for the sound of familiar footsteps. At six o'clock Dodd returned.

"Did you find the young preacher?" asked Emma.

"No, I didn't—I don't feel well."

"You are quite sick now, aren't you, Dear?"

"Yes, I guess I am. The pain is very severe." Oh, that wonderful heart. How much more could it take?

Emma went to the phone with pains of fear striking her own heart.

"His hands were so cold and clammy. Oh, if we were only home and I had his oxygen tent. If the doctor doesn't hurry, he will be gone before he gets here," she thought.

"Oh, dear Father in Heaven, ease his pain. I couldn't ask for any more— only Thy will be done. But thank you, Lord, just thank you for everything." Only the Father in heaven knew the pain in her own heart.

You couldn't live in harmony for so many years without feeling the turbulent thudding sound of discord when the "chimes" around which all your music revolved were not playing the same melody on your heartstrings. The pain and suffering was broken only by the ring of the bell.

"Come in, Doctor; we must do something—the pain is so severe."

"I am going to give him a hypodermic, Mrs. Dodd; that should ease him."

"Hello, Doctor. How are you?"

"Just great. I've been out on a fishing trip, Dr. Dodd."

"How many did you catch?

"I caught twenty—they were beauties!"

Dr. Dodd liked to fish, and despite his work and busy schedule, he always seemed to find time for his favorite pastime. Here he poses with a prize catch.

"How could they talk about a fishing trip at such a time?" cried Mrs. Dodd's heart; but another thought came simultaneously and helped to make her smile. Memories went back to a summer journey when they had taken Papa Dodd along. After days of seeing his son's passion for fishing at any opportunity, he said, "Emma, I believe if Elmon saw a tub of water on the roadside, he would fish in it."

"Ah, yes," she sighed. "How like him, even now. He does love to fish."

"I'll have to go now," the doctor said. "Have to go to another heart attack."

No oxygen tent; he kept right on suffering. Oh, the excruciating pain of watching a dear one agonize — helpless, except for prayer. Only God's all sufficient grace helps us endure the suffering of those so close who suffer.

The doctor called back to see if the pain had subsided.

"I'll send an ambulance right out, Mrs. Dodd."

"Sweetheart, they are coming to take you to the hospital."

"You won't leave me will you, Emma?"

"No, not for a second. I'll be right beside you."

From the very beginning, she had been right by his side—where else would you expect to find her now? It was nearing the hour of ten when they took him to St. Mary's Hospital and put him under an oxygen tent. The heartbeats were growing fainter and fainter; but, the great heart that had suffered so was still thinking of others.

"Mother, go pay the ambulance boys."

"I already have, Dear."

"But I wanted to give them a dollar extra apiece."

With the last words Mrs. Dodd ever heard him say, he was thinking of others; wanting to give them that extra something—even though suffering the agony and pain that only those know who have gone through the valley with a heart. He had preached the way of the Cross with every heartbeat. He had striven all his life to be more like Him. "See Jesus—not me," had been his humble plea. So conscious was he to obliterate self that he had a constant reminder before him every time he preached. The words on his pulpit, "We would see Jesus."

Now I ask you—how much like his Master could a humble servant of the Cross get? When suffering the agony of death—his last words and thoughts were of others.

"He's gone, Mrs. Dodd," said one of the nurses gently. "Come into this room and let me give you a hypodermic to ease the pain."

"Thank you, but I don't want that."

"But you must. You will need it."

"No, I won't. I will not take anything. I have someone standing by me that's better than that."

Praise God! She certainly did!

How could she tell them of the promise she and Dr. Dodd had made to each other that whichever one should go first that the other one would not take anything to knock them out?

"Why not?" you say.

This was their testimony—even in death, the Lord is sufficient for every need. If you do not have someone to stand by you in time of crisis, I recommend most profusely that you meet the Lord Jesus Christ. The man never lived that didn't need God at some time in his life to uphold and sustain. If that time hasn't come in your life, you may rest assured that it will. God can do without us, but we cannot do without God. And what is M. E. Dodd doing now? Why he's looking upon the face of the Son of God. And now that you've seen Him, what do you think, great heart?

"At my very best, I showed you only the twilight compared to His radiant presence."

"See, you didn't need to find that young preacher after all, now did you?"

"But Lord, the music. I did hear something this afternoon, didn't I? Why, there it is now."

The Lord just smiled as only He could smile on such a faithful servant who had preached Him and Him crucified all the days of his earthly life. As that smile continued, Dr. Dodd saw the reflection of the Glory of God shining through His Son, and heard the swelling of great music in tones so beautiful that it could not be equaled anywhere.

There was no mistake. He had heard music on earth that afternoon. Now he knew, that the angels had just been warming up to ring the bells of heaven. Yes, there was great rejoicing in heaven over the homecoming of this great servant of God. And herein lies the secret of his power. He was just that, a servant to all.

People couldn't receive a paper from the church or a man of the street couldn't pass by the giant structure without seeing the Scripture; that had been the motto of his very life. It permeated every nook and cranny of the great old church and the ends of the earth. "Not to be ministered unto; but to minister."

Did you listen?

Did you hear an echo? If you did, the Lord should have us all on our knees, praying, "O Father, just to be found faithful."

Is it worth it? We have seen the rewards. What will your choice be? No one can make it but you. My heart just cries out, "Oh Lord, give me another chance."

May this symphony of faith linger in your hearts and as we meet the Master each day; we can hear an echo saying—"Found faithful—found faithful—found faithful." Can you tell me anything you had rather have when you come to the gates of Glory than to hear the Master say, "Well done, my good and faithful servant"?

CHAPTER 14

Tablets of Stone

THE RAIN WAS FALLING SOFTLY AS WE DROVE TO THE airport to meet the plane which was bearing Dr. Dodd's body home. The windshield wipers sounded like clanging cymbals saying, "He's gone . . . He's gone."

Hundreds sadly stood like sentinels, awaiting the return of their "Sky Pilot" through chariots of clouds. So many times his people had met planes as Dr. and Mrs. Dodd returned from girdling the globe for God, but now, instead of that beaming smile and a wave of the hand—a stately coffin was lifted off the plane to the waiting hearse.

The silence drowned out all noise. Everyone and everything was motionless. Then one by one they filed away—each heart mourning, and their minds were vibrating chords of remembrance.

Shreveport stood still for the funeral. All stores were closed, and the people he had fought so hard in local option campaigns, parades, and speeches shut up shop! They knew he was a man of integrity and tested virtue. Yes, the doors of all the liquor stores were shut tight.

Inside the great old First Baptist Church at Travis and McNeil; you could hear the choir singing "One Day." It was Dr. Dodd's favorite hymn because he said it contained the whole gospel. I remember when we would sing it in a church service, and with those dancing blue eyes and the warm sunshine of a smile, he would say, "Sing it again—Sing it again."

> Living He loved me; dying He saved me,
> Buried He carried my sins far away;
> Rising He justified freely forever;
> One day He's coming—Oh, glorious day!

In 1955, three years after his death, Dr. Dodd was memorialized in Forest Park Cemetery with a marble replica of his pulpit from First Baptist Church of Shreveport.

At the funeral, Rowland Crowder, the associate pastor, prayed "Though he is not with us anymore, his deeds proclaim the gospel and even unto generations to come."

"It was Wednesday evening, August 6th, in the quiet stillness of a hospital room in Long Beach, California that Monroe Elmon Dodd, one of God's true and great servants, fell on sleep that his eyes might open on day dawn of that eternal morning. It is with solemn hush that we gather together in this place." These are the words that fell from the lips of Dr. James W. Middleton, pastor of the church. He had come in May—just two months before Dr. Dodd died. The church had been without a pastor for two years. You could admire the man—but filling his shoes came with another definition.

Dr. Middleton is still lifting his voice euphonically,

These comrades of the cross who have gathered across the land to pay honor and respect. I found in my own heart a deep sense of humility as one of the younger sons having stood in the shade of this giant oak in the forest of Christ's servants—to feel the touch of his hand as he wages conquest for Christ by the cross.—We pause to let our hearts have a fresh touch with the buoyant and optimistic soul who blazed a path across our time in great

service to our King. . . . preaching is the highest calling a man can have—
a great life telling a great truth. He spoke eloquently around the world, but
what he was, living and moving among us, spoke louder. It was worth the
man's salary just to have him walking the streets of our town.

Others spoke eloquently of Dr. Dodd's life.

Something above him and beyond him had laid hold on him that he
would not let go. There was a divine air about his mind and mood, a divine
air in the way he moved in the will of God, a divine impulse of divine will.

A humble lad from the hills of Tennessee placed his hand across contem-
porary Christian history in immortal tones and hues. We have lost from our
ranks a true and beloved pastor whom no one could replace. He moved
among his flock like a tender shepherd.

He was elder statesman and patriarch of the faith. Oft, the saints are
known better by the enemies they make than their friends. He was
unashamed to stand by that truth if he believed it to be right. He became
a spokesman for his people across the land. That great heart of his that
burned with a passion for lost souls led him on one missionary journey
after another and in him was his heart big enough for all the world.

He was divinely addicted—we hear of people being addicted to alcohol; he
was addicted to divine service. His great life pushed and drove him with
compassion clear to the end, when lesser souls would have fainted. Those that
remonstrated with him when he took his journey out west were reminded by
this giant of a man, "It's as near heaven from California as it is from Shreveport."

What must have been the greeting with George W. Truett, Sampey, Lee
Scarborough—and what must have been the golden convention their glad
hearts have had today; could wish for a triumphal blast, a trumpet, a shout
of song. One of God's great sons has gathered home. Help us to pick up the
torch he laid in our hands—give us some of his spirit.

Came spring as before, dressed in rich, rare apparel, and we found
ourselves basking in the shade of a lengthened shadow. It was May 9,
1955—five o'clock in the evening and people were gathered all around the
hill in Forest Park Cemetery for the unveiling and memorial service of the
monument that had been erected by friends and members of First Baptist
Church. It was an exact replica of the pulpit Dr. Dodd had preached from
for so many years detailed even to the "We would see Jesus" on the back; a
Bible on top with the first scripture he used in his first sermon on one side
and "For God so loved the World" on the other.

From the large platform that had been erected behind the monument, Dr. J. D. Grey, the main speaker, had just made a remark about the flying parson, a phrase that had been used in other days when preachers hadn't even thought of flying. He went on to say,

> People are known by whom they delight to be made known, you are honored because you honor him. This stone is so appropriate here crowning this hill with those asleep waiting for the resurrection. In Denmark, I was elected to succeed Dr. Dodd on the Executive Committee. I carried the sad news into Nigeria and other countries. Down in Nigeria when I told the African preachers, they broke into sobs and cried aloud.

On February 22, 1952, he left a note [to Grey] which read, "It is my wish that you preach my funeral, only refer to me to point to some spiritual truth or lesson, but do not leave an important engagement to do it." This note was not found until after his funeral, but perhaps it was just as well, because Dr. Dodd would not have wanted Dr. Grey to come home from overseas, and it was good that his heart did not have to make this decision.

Dr. Grey's words continued.

> Their works do follow them. If you would see his monument, look about you, living epistles, you are the living work. I speak for ministers of the Cross; one thing that would characterize him would be standing in the pulpit. His unyielding devotion to the word of God was the most remarkable thing about him.
>
> In city and political life, he was outstanding. On M. E. Dodd Day, civic leaders and all men's clubs paid him tribute. Protestant, Catholic, Jews alike came by to pay homage. He was Shreveport's first citizen. He was not narrow—he was a world citizen. His outreach ministry to the ends of the earth made you known all over the world. If it hadn't been for his going, you would never have been honored. Children, yet unborn will view this and know that here was one who proclaimed the gospel.

Jones Brothers Company, Inc., who made the monument, said it well when they wrote, "It is seldom that we have an opportunity to work on a memorial of such intricate design and proportion. The individual to whom this memorial is placed must have had a tremendous meaning in the community in which he lived."

Charles Forbes Taylor, the evangelist, came to the original pulpit from which the replica was copied and said,

> No matter what happens in the great old First Baptist Church, the length-ening shadow of Dr. M. E. Dodd will always be felt there. Once I heard a voice over the air and thought that it sounded like someone I knew; then, I heard him say, "Lord Jesus Christ," and I said, "That's M. E. Dodd. No one ever said the Lord Jesus Christ like he did.
>
> I stood with him when he was preaching in the great Temple Church in California. We had a great service and many men had walked the aisles who were hardened sinners. When he was finished, he turned around and said, "Well, Charlie, that's one more day's work for Jesus and one less for me."

I hear the chimes ringing gloriously again throughout the city. I see men with heads upturned knowing there is deity. The chimes of Shreveport I see as he walked among men. Not to be ministered unto, but to minister, he said again and again. Doesn't that make the chimes ring within your heart and want to let Jesus there His grace impart? Save yourself—others you cannot save, so here you have the secret of the chimes way. If I am to ring the bells so others may see, I must give myself completely to Thee.

CHAPTER 15

*These Also
Are Called*

MY MOTHER TOLD ME A STORY FROM HER CHILDHOOD
that relates to the life of a preacher's wife. "When I was a girl of twelve, we
had a visiting minister and his wife for Sunday dinner. (Mother's papa was a
preacher.) The discussion came around to the dress of preachers' wives, and
the visiting preacher said apologetically, 'Some seem to think that my wife
dresses a little too showy.' No sooner had these words flowed quiescently
from his lips, than this lovely petite woman took her fists and hit her husband
in the chest as hard as she could—so hard, in fact, that the poor man started
coughing, and nearly lost his breath."

"You weren't a preacher when I married you," she stated vehemently, "so,
I'm not called to the ministry!"

As my mother cautiously shared this experience with me, it was obvious
that she was not sure if she should speak so disparagingly about such a delicate subject. However, she went on to explain how she had spoken up and
said, "I thought preachers' wives were called too."

"No!" the woman answered emphatically. "They are not!"

"This made a profound impression on me," Mother said, "one which I
have never forgotten."

So much could be said on this subject, but I shall restrain myself, and
say only enough to set the stage for Emma Savage Dodd. This is her
chapter; she is the star. It is also for my mother and all my dear friends who
are preachers' wives.

Our mission board would not think of sending out missionaries if the
wife did not feel called also, but every church is one of God's mission
fields. Some women really do receive a special call, but all preachers' wives
do whether they are aware of it or not. If a man is not a preacher when he

120

marries, but is called to the ministry later in life, God is not just calling the man; He is also calling his wife.

The biography of a great man is incomplete without at least a chapter on his wife, but I can understand why authors steer away from this subject many times; there is very little to be found about them. My mentor, Richard Ellsworth Day, had this problem when he was writing about Emma Moody and Susannah Spurgeon. He was appalled at the dearth of information—sometimes only a paragraph. Although this chapter is devoted to Emma Savage Dodd, her footprints are all through this book.

I have had the privilege of knowing many wonderful preachers. Some achieved great things for the Lord in spite of their wives. But I have also seen many who were crippled because their wives were not in sympathy with their calling.

Emma always wanted to marry a preacher, and wanted him to have a wonderful library like her father. She also felt called to be a missionary when she was a young girl; so, she was more than ready and equipped when the time came for her to leave on her honeymoon with her dashing young preacher husband.

Mrs. Dodd, like so many preachers' wives, could have gone anywhere in the world and done her own thing. She was well educated, talented, and at ease in any circle. She was an outstanding artist with many beautiful paintings to her credit. Those which hang in the homes of her children and grandchildren would be worthy of anyone's gaze. My favorite is a portrait of "Ruth and Naomi" which now hangs in the home of the Hubert Joyners—their granddaughter. The story of Ruth also bespeaks of the way she felt about M. E. D.: "Entreat me not to leave thee or return from following after thee. For whither thou goest, I will go, and where thou lodgest, I will lodge. Thy people shall be my people and thy God my God. Whither thou dies, I will die, there will I be buried." This was her theme song throughout her life; there was never any doubt that she made melodious the life of the one by her side—he was the "Chimes."

One fine piece written in the Silver Anniversary edition on M. E. D. intricately paints her portrait:

> In order to achieve success, one must be willing to sacrifice in order that others may succeed. Such has been the life of Mrs. M. E. Dodd. Through all the eventful years of her husband's ministry, she has been his loyal and faithful companion, sharing his sorrows and joys, helping him in the bearing

of burdens, reinforcing him in the hour of discouragement, and pointing the way with her simple faith.

She is a sweet-spirited woman of great ability. She is the queen of her home over which she presides with grace and dignity. They have been blessed with five children—Dorothy, Helen, Martha, Monroe Elmon Jr., and Lucille.

While mentioning the children, let me interject something here close to humanity, lest I lead you to believe that the bells never rang out of tune. The Dodds thought travel was educational for their children. "I don't know how educational it was for them, but it certainly was for me," Mrs. Dodd said—getting clothes ready for five children and trying to keep up with them. Dr. Dodd always got a seven-passenger touring car for these trips. Lucille walked all the way to Washington one year—at least she claimed she did! The children would get hot in the back of the car, and it was like a nest of hornets. Dr. Dodd made whoever started the fuss get out and walk awhile. Apparently, Lucille always started the fuss or got blamed. She did indeed walk most of the time, but the car would go slow enough so she could keep up. Such family interaction can't help but bring a smile to any father and mother who have traveled with children before the days of air conditioning and freeway traffic.

In talking to Dr. Dodd about the writing of the chimes, I asked him if the children ever bothered him when he studied at home. "No, never," he answered. "I had such deep concentration that the noise or running never distracted me."

When asked about her childhood, Emma said that she was a quiet child who liked to read a lot. "Mother would read to us at night, and I always got a book for Christmas. I was the favorite of my brother George Savage who was an ear, eye, nose, and throat specialist in Memphis.

"I was one of ten children—third of ten. Mother reared three girls that were not hers—nine girls and one boy. When I got married, I always wanted someone who could give me all the salmon salad sandwiches I wanted. I loved them and could never get enough with ten children."

Emma's mother, Fanny Savage, was the daughter of a wealthy planter. She was offered a place as teacher of Latin at Mary Charlotte College in Winchester, Tennessee. However, her father wanted her to leave that open for some young woman who had to make her way. There were so few jobs for women at that time. She fell and broke her hip when she was sixty, and it left her crippled for the rest of her life; but, she went right on, and taught the Fanny Savage Sunday School Class. They had a special chair built for her from which she could teach at First Baptist Church, Jackson, Tennessee. During the worship service, she sat in her chair at the front of the church. After she died, they left it there for a long time.

Emma's father, Dr. George Savage, was a great man of prayer, and early in life she was conscious of this power. "He also had little cards all over the house reading, 'Children should be seen and not heard.' With ten, I thought, you needed all the help you could get." Dr. Savage liked to help young preachers. He would bring chickens and eggs home from the churches where he would preach on the weekends and feed them to the preacher boys. People were always getting on him for doing this; they knew he could easily use it all himself. He also gave them jobs around the house in the summer to help them earn money for their tuition for the next year.

Dr. Savage served at Union University in Jackson, Tennessee for over fifty years. What a temptation it would be right now to say more; worthy, no doubt, is this man's life. But just permit me a line or two of the meteoric life of this man that speaks for itself.

On the old campus of Union University, there is a memorial tree which was planted in honor of Dr. Savage — an inscription in stone near the base of the tree reads:

Cedar of Lebanon
Grand Old Tree of the Bible
Planted in Memory of
Union's Grand Old Man
Doctor Savage
May 1, 1947

This tree is brilliantly lighted every year the last three weeks in December as Union's Christmas tree. On the new campus, there is the George Savage Chapel. The school moved in 1975; they also moved the memorial stone. His works did follow him. Such was the heritage of Emma Savage Dodd. What better mold could this clay have come from? When the lambent flame of divine glory fell on the shoulders of M. E. Dodd, there is no doubt that God gave Emma to him to help keep that flame aglow.

In the centennial history of First Baptist Church, there is a glowing column on Emma Savage Dodd. Her achievements would pale those of many a man. Shall I list them for you? No! I must acquiesce to what I feel would be Emma's decision; you will have to do your own research. I must use this space to say what I think would please her the most. The church said, "Her ideal life has been her husband's inspiration for she has helped to make him an outstanding minister and world leader among Baptists for the cause of Christ."

A GREAT SOUL PASSES

There are many reviews about the Dodds in magazines and papers across the land, but a simple little one-page Sunday School newsletter from one of the men's Bible classes portrays her in the most vivid color.

> Our hearts were saddened a few days ago by the passing of a great soul who never claimed membership in our class, but touched the lives of most of us. We are referring of course to Mrs. M. E. Dodd, wife of our former beloved pastor, and mother of some of our finest members. We wonder how many of our members will recall the sweet-faced little lady who always made an effort to accompany her great husband when he performed a wedding ceremony, or who stood at the bedside of so many of our own mothers, wives and sisters as they slipped from this earth to join our Heavenly Father?
>
> God blessed her home with several fine children, but she always found time to look after her "church family" also, and for many years, she was the teacher of our sweethearts, mothers, wives, and sisters in one of our largest women's Sunday School classes. Only her failing health forced her to give up this most important task. We can still see her in later years, after the departure of her great companion, quietly sitting on the left-hand side of our sanctuary, always ready with a sweet smile of greeting for those who stopped for a little chat. God truly touched her life in a wondrous way, and all of us can say in all sincerity—Gone, but not forgotten.

What Dr. Dodd said about her could have been the whole chapter, and it would have spoken volumes. His testimony of Emma was that her prayer life had been a source of unfailing blessing to him in his work. Did you hear that? Doesn't it just make you want to fall on your knees? A thousand bells are ringing from the tower so tall. Could prayer have made the Chimes ring?

I went to see Mrs. Dodd one day a good while after the angels had taken M. E. D. to his heavenly home. She said two very simple things that had a profound effect on my life, and maybe they can mean something in yours. She was in a wheelchair now, and unable to get out. The years were advancing, and her little shoulders were bent. "You know," she said, "we lived such a full life with the demands of a large church, convention, and world travels. There were many times I wished I could stay home, but now that I can't go, I would give anything if I could." Then she looked away and said, "I have million dollar memories."

She shared one short anecdote with me that was so befitting of this couple:

"I remember Dr. Dodd came home one day, and I told him that I had heard from the children. He looked at me and said, 'Have you heard from God today?' I was rather taken back; then, I realized he was speaking of God's love letter to us—the Bible."

Dear friend, have you heard from God today?

So the little girl that was born May 1, 1878, and died April 2, 1960, was now laid to rest beside her husband, and what great thing was on her tombstone? Just her name, date of birth, and death. But this was fitting too; for there was the beautiful monument that friends and church members had erected for Dr. Dodd, a replica of his pulpit—his honor and praise were her praise too; for she sought no renown for herself.

She had been by his side in life, and now was at his side again, and that's all she ever wanted to be. Let me say just one more thing even though I do it with great reluctance. I believe that great numbers of you deep down in your hearts would agree that when we get to heaven, the Lord will probably place more stars in the crowns of faithful preachers' wives than all the honored, and much-written-about husbands. Such a one will be Emma Savage Dodd.

Ring out again, oh bells. They were one! So, she too is the Chimes!

Chapter 16

Lagniappe

IF THIS IS NEW TO YOU, JUST SAY, "LAN — YAP," AND YOU WILL be in Louisiana. If you are a customer making a purchase, the tradesman might give you a demitasse-size present or something extra. It is a Haitian Creole word — a mainspring of the Pelican State. So, here is your lagniappe from the life of M. E. Dodd — something "extra," gems, if you please.

Firsts are worthy of being remembered; because, when you launch the first step or lay the first stone under God's call and guidance, you are blazing a trail and breaking paths for others to follow. When the seed is planted and grows into the calendar of time, we can walk with a lighter foot because the ground has been broken. Even though it may be a mote of dust, we will fruitify until the fields are covered with verdant grass and bricks and steeples will rise for the glory of God. Here are some firsts from the life of M. E. Dodd.

- First Baptist Church, Shreveport, has the distinction of being first in the United States to install a radio broadcasting station of its own. The broadcasts from the pulpit lasted from 7:45 to 9:30 every Sunday evening (including the regular sermons), and the last thirty minutes were devoted to a feature program in which Dr. Dodd answered questions from his congregation and radio listeners. Through this channel over station KWKH, he was able to speak from two to five million people every Sunday night.
- 1938 — First all-airplane tour of all the Americas covering 18,000 miles.
- 1934 — First World Mission Tour.
- First to be known as the "Flying Parson" — headlining newspapers.
- First president of the Southern Baptist Convention to make it more than a title by traveling all over the land.
- Dr. Dodd began the Pastors' Conference before the meeting of the Convention.

- First Baptist Hour Speaker.
- Dr. Dodd was the chosen leader of monumental efforts of Southern Baptists that are woven throughout the book.

Dr. Dodd set the machinery in motion to lead the way—unfurled his wings to sow the seeds of the Lord Jesus Christ. Listen and you can almost hear the bells of history clanging against the metal. Now is the all-glorious appointed hour. Which hour? The Baptist Hour. The year—1941.

"We are coming to you from the auditorium of First Baptist Church, Shreveport. We present the first in a series of thirteen programs sponsored by the radio committee of the Southern Baptist Convention. The theme is 'The Living Christ in the World of Today.' The speaker for this first Baptist Hour is Dr. M. E. Dodd."

The years marched by, and we found ourselves in 1991. Blazoned across the front of the *Shreveport Times* in full color are the churchgoers of First Baptist Church celebrating the longevity of this swinging pendulum of time: "Baptist Hour Turns 50—Giving the Winds a Mighty Voice" was the theme. They brought in the same pulpit from which Dr. Dodd delivered "Christ and Human Crises" in 1941. That year had marked the dawn of a new day in proclamation of the gospel. Through the technology of recording, the Good News had become available to a vast audience undreamed of at that time. Dr. Dodd's 1941 message was timely because the United States was on the verge of World War II. By 1991, five hundred radio stations carried the program along with the American Christian Television System.

Seconds fly on wings and the moving fingers of time say it is 2001—sixty years of the Baptist Hour. Let us keep it a majestic stream gliding to the ocean of eternity.

Dr. Dodd's Ideas On Ordination

Jesus is Lord supremely in the religious kingdom. He is the sole mediator between God and man. We will bow the knee and humble the heart and bend the will to none other. Any man who in the holy moment of ordination falls upon His knees and agrees to preach any other preaching than that which the Lord Jesus bids him preach surrenders the holiest rights of a human soul and violates the first principle of religious life. Let Jesus alone be Lord of all because He is as high above all others as the "pyramids are above the sands of the desert."

The racing engine of my brain went immediately to 1 Corinthians 9:16. "Woe is me if I preach not the gospel." Let us always call to remembrance — a strong and faithful pulpit is the safeguard of a nation's life.

Dr. Dodd's Funniest Experiences

I was preaching in a large fashionable church in Florida. The warm sunlit day was in such contrast to the state from which I had come that following the morning service and lunch, I sat in the yard near the water all afternoon. To protect my eyes while reading, I used a visor. When I went into the house to prepare for the evening worship service, I was horrified at myself in the mirror. From where the visor rested on my forehead, the bald pate was red as a beet and from where it shaded my face just under my nose was as red as fire. The shaded part of my face was a white streak. I looked like a clown at a circus. Horrors! How could I ever face that aristocratic congregation? My hostess had the answer with a liberal supply of cosmetics. She rouged the white streak and powdered the red into a perfect blend. I looked like a prima-donna as I ascended the pulpit with great confidence. But when I got to preaching with all of my vim, vigor, and enthusiasm, a bit of perspiration broke out on my forehead and when I used my handkerchief, the powder came off leaving a fiery red spot exposed. I observed a worried look on the face of the congregation. When perspiration reached my cheeks, I wiped it off exposing the ghostly white, which triggered a burst of snickers from the young people. Within a few minutes, the make-up was gone and the whole congregation was in an uproar. All I could do was to ask them to stand for the benediction.

Before the days of air-conditioned churches, I was preaching on a hot summer evening in a village church in Tennessee. Just as I went into the pulpit, a lovely lady with all kindness and grace handed me a split bamboo fan. I began preaching and fanning. Occasionally, I would gesture with the fan straight up in the air. I noticed the eyes of many people following the fan with intense interest. Some of the men would draw their hand across their mouth. When the service ended, a number rushed up and demanded to know what I was being paid to advertise that business. I looked at the fan and for the first time saw the words — Anhauser Busch Company, Bottled and Keg Beer.

Quotable Quotes

Dr. Dodd was speaking to a group of medical students. "You haven't studied enough until you find God in it all," he said.

CHICAGO DAILY NEWS—AUGUST 13, 1933

Famous Baptist Pastor Preaches Here Sunday—Large crowds are expected both tomorrow morning and evening at the Second Baptist Church, Jackson Boulevard and Lincoln Street, to hear sermons by the Rev. M. E. Dodd, D. D., pastor of the First Baptist Church of Shreveport, La. Dodd is president of the Southern Baptist Convention, representing more than 4,000,000 Baptists.

1926 SCRAPBOOK

The *Herald Democrat,* Trenton, Tenn.—Union University Gives LL.D. Degree to Dr. M. E. Dodd.

Dr. and Mrs. M. E. Dodd returned Thursday morning from Jackson, Tenn., where they attended the commencement of Union University, which conferred the degree of LL.D. upon Dr. Dodd. President H. E. Waters of the university conferred the degree upon the unanimous recommendation of faculty and board of trustees by the gift of the hood which signifies by its colors of purple and red the LL.D. degree.

Dr. Dodd received his Bachelor of Arts degree and Bachelor of Oratory degree from Union University in 1904. Baylor University conferred the Doctor of Divinity degree in 1918.

The Spirit-Filled Life

To be filled with the Holy Spirit is also a power to be utilized. Many church members plod wearily along at their irksome and sometimes irritating tasks. This is because they are working in the energy of the flesh instead of in the power of the Spirit. Divine provision, abundant and sufficient, has been made for all that they require for doing God's work. And if they would only tap the resources of that inexhaustible reservoir, they would find powers released to them of which they had never dreamed—and then they would accomplish superhuman exploits of faith." M. E. Dodd

Virtue of Vision

Whereupon, O King Agrippa, I was not disobedient unto the Heavenly Vision," Acts 26:19.

The first virtue of vision is the vitality which it produces for creative thinking and constructive service. The lack of vision produces inertia, disinterest, and destruction. Solomon said, "Where there is no vision, the people perish."

Vision is a gift of God, and it is a very deep reality. It comes from the presence of the Holy Spirit in the heart . . .

Vision is the ability to recognize spiritual resources, values and forces beyond and above the material things which may be seen with the natural eye. It is idealism in contrast to materialism . . . Vision does not mean vain fantasies nor does it mean some beatific and ecstatic experience. It means to be intelligently conscious of opportunities lying ahead, of resources by which to accomplish those opportunities, which the near-sighted and the materialist do not see.

All The People Stood Up

And in Nehemiah we read—"And when he opened the book, all the people stood up." It was a request as well as a comand—the congregation stood as one likened to a military review. We stood as if electrified, but rose with honor standing at attention to hear the word of God. The voice was the timbre of a singing wire, as well as liquid music. Many came from miles around just to hear Dr. Dodd read the scripture and let Jesus into their hearts. Yes, when he opened the Bible all the people stood up. When Dr. Dodd prayed, the people felt they were reaching the eternal home of heaven. As he lifted up his voice, it had all consuming and embracing power coupled with compassionate pathos. At the close of each of Dr. Dodd's prayers, his voice would drop to half a gale and you could hear, "Heal the sick, Lift up the fallen, Care for the dying, Save the lost, Bring us all to Thyself in Glory, Through Jesus Christ, our Lord, Amen!" As he voiced each need, beseeching the Lord, you could feel the Master's hand on each momentous situation. As his voice lifted, you could feel waves of music flowing into your soul as Dr. Dodd prayed to the King—the King of Kings.

1911—MAIDEN ADDRESS TO SOUTHERN BAPTIST CONVENTION

It was in denominational service that Dr. Dodd did the thing which unwittingly but providentially led him to Shreveport and the pastorate of the First Baptist Church. Another periodical brought its pen to life when he had been at First Baptist Church for thirty-five years.

At the Southern Baptist Convention, Jacksonville, Florida, in 1911, Dr. Dodd, then a messenger from Kentucky, made his maiden address to the convention. His topic was "Mountain Schools," a denominational project conducted by the Baptist Home Mission Board in the vastness of the Kentucky, Tennessee, and North Carolina mountains. It was from such schools that came many Baptist leaders, including the late Dr. George W. Truett of Dallas, Texas and Dr. F. C. McConnell of Atlanta, Georgia.

At the time, First Baptist Church, Shreveport was virtually without the services of a minister, as its pastor, Dr. Henry A. Sumrell was in failing health. He died a few months later.

Sitting in the convention audience when Dr. Dodd spoke were two messengers from the Shreveport church. They were T. R. Lawhon and Dr. C. C. McCloud. Dr. Dodd delivered such a forceful address that it made a deep impression upon the Shreveport messengers. During the address, Dr. McCloud nudged Lawhon and said, "That's our next pastor."

Dr. Dodd did not meet the messengers from Shreveport, nor did he know anything at the time of the impression he had made. Months later, after the death of Dr. Sumrell, he received a call from the Shreveport church and after prayer and deliberation, accepted.

That was one of the great milestones in his life. For 35 years, Shreveport was the base and First Baptist Church, the inspiration for his notable nation-wide and global ministries for the kingdom of God.

1913—NEW INNOVATION

On February 2, 1913, the church voted to install telephone extensions to enable shut-ins to hear the sermons each Sunday. This was the forerunner of the days of radio.

FIRST TIME ON THEIR KNEES

In 1915, Dr. Dodd addressed the Southern Baptist Convention for the second time. This year they were meeting in Houston, Texas, and his topic was "The Prayer Life of Jesus," which became the title of a book written by him. It was at this convention that Dr. Dodd introduced an innovation by calling on all the messengers to kneel in prayer. Old convention messengers recall the incident and humorously remark that it was the "first time a Baptist convention ever got on its knees for anybody and this time, only to God."

STAY TWO YEARS

When the Dodds had been in Shreveport for thirty-five years, the *Shreveport Times* lured Mrs. Dodd into print from a human standpoint. They had just left a congregation of eighteen hundred at Louisville, Kentucky, to come to a church with 582 members. When you are going to receive less, it is really God's call! Emma said, "I'll stay here just two years to satisfy you, but then, I'm ready to pack and go anywhere else."

"You could hardly blame her," Dr. Dodd says, "because Shreveport then was just a hick Red River town." Ramshackle cafes and garages lined Texas Avenue. There was no South Highlands, Cedar Grove, Queensborough, Broadmoor, and Bossier City was just a few timber buildings. The streets were nearly all unpaved. At the intersection of Kings Highway and Fairfield Avenue was a trail for horseback riders.

"I've seen the city grow from a small river town to a thriving and still expanding metropolis, and my congregation grew from 582 to 5,421," said Dr. Dodd.

"Shreveport was Mrs. Dodd's life and leaving never entered her mind again," wrote the *Times* staff writer.

GLOBE-TROTTING

Dr. Dodd's congregation had been sympathetic to his globe-trotting proclivities, for the members knew that they and all Christendom would reap the benefits. It explains, too, why on Sundays the great auditorium of his church was filled to overflowing.

Baptists were not any different in the 1930s than they are today. They wanted their pastor at home, but realized he was unique in his calling from God and no one else could make the paths that he must trod. However, Dr. Dodd knew people and was a genius for that time at being at his church when he was gone. He had codes for his staff, deacons, and family. These would go on telegrams he would send to cut cost. He also spoke at all the services when he was gone for great lengths of time. The congregation heard their pastor over an electric transcription radio broadcast. Yes, they were with him everywhere he went.

IN DEBT

In the midst of the depression in 1933, Dr. Dodd assumed the presidency of the Southern Baptist Convention and found the financial affairs in dire

During their 1934 mission tour, Dr. and Mrs. Dodd (front row, holding child) visited Japan, where they met with Toyohiko Kagawa. A popular Japanese magazine of the time dubbed Kagawa (glasses, front row) one of Japan's two greatest living men, and he was known as the greatest Christian of his time. An Army official was the other.

straits with debts of over $6,500,000. For three years, he preached, pleaded, and prayed, "Owe no man anything."

The convention heard and heeded, and methods were adopted and carried out which finally paid every debt with interest without defaulting a single penny.

1934 — AMBASSADORS FOR BAPTISTS

At the close of the 1934 session of the Baptist World Alliance, moreover, Dr. and Mrs. Dodd determined to carry out their plans, to "girdle the globe for God," and to actually visit all the main Baptist mission stations in Europe, Palestine, India, China, and Japan. During this world-girdling tour, Dr. Dodd was privileged to hold personal interviews with David Lloyd George of England; Mahatma Gandhi of India; the Grand Mufti in Jerusalem; Mrs. SunYat Sen and her son, Dr. Sun Fo of China; also with Toyohiko Kagawa of Japan, Baron Yaskawa of Japan; also with Dr. H. H. Kung and Dr. Herman C. E. Liu of China. Altogether, his trip and conferences covered four continents and eighteen nations and took him and Mrs. Dodd over 32,000 miles. The whole story of this amazing missionary tour of the nations is told in Dr. Dodd's book, *Girdling the Globe for God.*

CALLED A DOLLAR MARK

Such criticism has never fazed Dr. Dodd in his work. The liberal giver never criticizes; the critic rarely ever gives liberally. It is not selfishness to ask for money for the church or benevolent causes.

Let the carping critics cast their barbs and the cynics hurl their bans, Dr. Dodd had no apologies for his position on the matter of money. He learned its value by hard experience on the farm, at a lumber mill, in college, and through inspiration in the service of God. He knew that a dollar spent in the church is the best investment in the world. He pointed out that twenty-seven of the twenty-nine parables of Jesus deal with the subject of money and that money used in mission work brings about material as well as spiritual profit.

John Dillinger, whom J. Edgar Hoover went after back in the 1930s, cost the American people $3,000,000. What if a missionary had reached Dillinger to divert his career into decent channels?

Dr. Dodd knew the value of money. He knew its worth and its important place in the work of God's kingdom. He always spoke of money as "coined character" and "concentrated consecration to Christ and the Church."

SPORTS

From childhood, M. E. Dodd was athletically inclined, and he attributed his splendid health and physique largely to his devotion to sports. As he neared the three-score-and-ten milestone, he was able to work hard each day, eat heartily, and sleep soundly. A day's traveling, fishing, or hard work did not exhaust him any more than it did men many years his junior. In 1945 he traveled 35,000 miles, spoke 450 times to over 2,000,000 people, and produced and distributed over 8,500,000 pages of literature.

All clean sports are not only good for the physical man but for the spiritual man as well. For this reason, Dr. Dodd was an ardent devotee of sports all of his life. Also, he was able on many occasions to use his love of sports for the glory of God—his famous fishing sermon was always in demand.

DODD AND THE HECKLER

A 1947 article from the *St. Louis Post Dispatch*—"Baptist Heckler called to order." The paper showed a picture of Dr. Dodd pointing a finger at J. Frank Norris ordering him to cease his heckling.

Norris would use a loudspeaker on the outside, then go inside and continue in his notorious ways. No one knew who called them, but sometimes police officers would appear on the scene.

The incident was also mentioned in *Time*, 1947 — "The presiding minister Dr. M. E. Dodd of Shreveport, Louisiana raised a forbidding hand, but Norris had already started in his high strident voice. Desperately, Dr. Dodd fell back on the pastor's last resort: he raised his voice and sang, 'How Firm a Foundation.' The congregation loyally joined in, but grinning Heckler Norris was right with them."

TO THE DOWN AND OUT

Let us turn from the scenes in Kaiserdam Hall and the crowd at the Hall of Religion and see Dr. Dodd in places more humble, more squalid, but equally dramatic. The scene is down on Shreveport's riverfront amid the shacks of the shabby, the places of the poor, the sordidness of sin. It is the water's edge where the dens of the destitute and the haunts of hell are thrown together in helter-skelter fashion, creating a jungle of ugliness.

With the smoke that rises from the shambles is mingled the acrid and fetid odors of a city dumping ground. Yonder stands a fisherman's shack with its offensive smells.

Nearby stands a "dragline" rusting since its last excavating duty, and the boats of those who harvest catfish are locked to the shore. It is evening, and the weary day is over for those who eke out their living by tempting these denizens of the deep with bits of blood bait on fishhooks. Over to the side stands a dilapidated freight car, its days of practical service over, and it has been removed from the railroad switch to the graveyard of obsolete boxcars amid this scene of decaying things — animal, vegetable, and human.

But look! Something has happened to that old boxcar! There are steps leading to its wide door and there are people inside. Shabbily dressed people, of course — shirt-sleeved, barefooted, disheveled — but people just the same, human souls for whom Jesus died. Inside are huddled forty men, women, and children — the car's capacity. Outside, unable to find space within, stand half a dozen or more of these derelicts — people of the Red River batture — the habitues of the slums. Here reside the "river rats" as some of these folks are derisively named because they toil not; neither do they eat regularly. Listen! You can hear, coming from the boxcar, unfurled voices and sounds of "Jesus Saves" and "Just as I Am." A balding man rises to speak. He reverently opens his Bible and says, "Let us hear the word of God." His voice rings through the

Child piano prodigy Van Cliburn poses with Dr. Dodd during a riverfront mission in Shreveport (circa 1939). Cliburn and his family attended First Baptist, and Van Cliburn frequently performed at the church.

ramshackle boxcar. It is the same voice that in infancy cried in western Tennessee. It is the same resonant voice that brought thousands in Kaiserdam Hall to their feet in applause. It is the same voice that rang out to 90,000 from the Hall of Religion in New York. It is the same voice that told millions of the glory of God, the saving grace of Jesus Christ and here, tonight, it brings the same message to the hovels of the hungry, the shacks of the shabby and to the souls that are lost. In Kaiserdam Hall the inspiration had been great, and at the Hall of Religion there was power in his words. But tonight at this humble place in the midst of underprivileged people, Dr. Dodd felt, as he had never felt before, the presence and the power of the Holy Spirit. On other occasions, he had felt the inspiration of multitudes; tonight, he felt the glorified presence of the One who said, "I will be with you." The gospel of Jesus Christ, which is the good news of love, life, and liberty, finds its way with equal power and effect into the hearts of all people in all places. "It matters not," says Dr. Dodd, "what may be a man's race, tongue, or nationality; the power of Christianity to change life, character, and conduct works in the hearts of each with equal force. The human heart is moved alike, be it Oriental or Occidental."

On the day of his fiftieth anniversary as a minister of the gospel and thirty-eighth anniversary as pastor of First Baptist Church, Shreveport, Louisiana, Dr. Dodd said, "I have envied no man his gold, his rank, his power, and if I had it to do all over again, I would still go the way of the cross."

Postlude

WHO ARE YOU?

From the capital of Japan—Tokyo, the city of cherry blossoms in the spring and lotus blossoms in the summer—you could feel God's presentation of beauty in all of its glory! It was October 14, 1964, and the Summer Olympics, which began in 1896, were in full swing. It was a cosmopolitan crowd from all parts of the world.

Billy Mills, a twenty-six-year-old Marine lieutenant—an orphan and Native American—had taken up running and was entering the 10,000-meter run—a six-mile race. No American had ever come close to winning a gold medal in that category. Most of them ran short distances.

The race started—each participant trying to crack all records. Clarke took the early lead, chased by previous Olympians Petr Bolotnikov of Russia, Murray Hallberg of New Zealand, future Olympic medalist Mamo Wolde of Ethiopia, and Mohamed Gammoudi of Tunisia. Mills managed to keep pace with the chase pack. Several times during the race, Clarke put on a burst of speed as to fly on the wings of the wind to distance himself from the field, but each time Mills caught up with him, sometimes taking the lead. Gradually, other runners fell back and out of the race. Only Clarke, Gammoudi, and Mills stayed in front.

At the beginning of the race's final lap, each runner prepared to make his move to take the lead. Clarke moved first, sidestepping another runner on the track and bumping into Mills in the process. Seeing the collision, Gammoudi surged forward between the two, brushing against both runners and taking the lead. He could hear sheer pandemonium breaking out in the stands—wild disorder—tumult—and could hear with the pound of each step, "He's going to win, he's going to win; he's copped the prize."

But wait, wait!! Clarke regained stride and closed on Gammoudi; however, it was Mills who had the most power left in his sprint. He turned on a burst of speed and annihilated space completely. You could hear the roar of the crowd even now—perpetual, incessant, and majestic.

Here he comes! Here he comes! U.S.A. and #722 emblazoned on his chest. Just a few meters from the finish line, Mills took the lead, breaking the tape just four-tenths of a second in front of second place Gammoudi. It was an astonishing surprise to everyone. He not only shocked himself, but also the world. He was surrounded with a halo—basking in the sunshine of fame. If you looked hard enough, you could see the American spirit embedded at the top of the flag. No American had ever won the 10,000 meter Olympic gold medal, and no one even considered Mills would come close.

Even more unbelievable was Mills's Olympic record time of 28:24.4, an astonishing 45.6 seconds faster than he had ever run before in this event. Billy Mills came into the Olympics as an unknown athlete, but he left an American hero. In the 104 years of the Summer Olympics, no American has broken his record.

Nineteen years after he took the gold medal, the movie *Running Brave* was released, chronicling his life and inspirational Olympic achievement. When the race was over, the press and the crowd were so shocked that Billy was stopped from running the traditional victory lap. A Japanese official from the press box ran up to him, and with the sound of fanfare in the air, raised his voice cannonlike and said in disbelief, "Who are you?"

Billy Graham said, "We are put on the earth to glorify God." Who are you? "Seek ye first the Kingdom of God." Who are you? "Bring ye all the tithes into the storehouse." Who are you? "Do unto others as you would have them do unto you." Who are you? "Love your neighbor as yourself." Who are you? "Go ye into all the world and preach the gospel." Who are you? "For God so loved the world that He gave His only begotten Son; that whosoever believeth in Him should not perish but have everlasting life." Who are you?

"Oh dear Lord, this author and your servant has fallen short of these words, 'Who are you?' so many times. So, who am I, Lord—who am I?"

He answered, "I have called you by name, you are mine."

Jesus Christ is at the finish line waiting for you to break the tape. If you do, your name will be written in the record book of all record books. Is your name written there?

GOD LEADS HIS DEAR CHILDREN

My preacher husband could fling up a song like a curve of gold. It was a thrilling sound and was heard with his Chimesmen recording quartet at our Southern Baptist Convention. I can still hear the lift of his voice in the old hymn, "God Leads His Dear Children Along":

> Some through the waters
> Some through the flood
> Some through the fire
> But all through the blood.
> Some through great sorrow,
> But God gives the song
> In the night season and all the day long.

No matter how sinuous the road, God is always there to give the song. This is my final curtain — my epilogue. The last note has been played . . .

Let the music linger.

Appendix

ON THE DODD TRAIL—NOTES FROM MY SKETCHBOOK

1987—California: I came once again to where his footprints last trod—to feel the last walk to eternity and to notice the feet never stopped walking until stilled by His Maker—but the prints remain. Ah, the blueprints on which we must forever build. What a heritage is ours!

Oh where do you go, footprints on the sands of time? Do the waves come and wash away all evidence of the steps set in?

No! It reaches a crescendo all powerful, and is set forever in the concrete of our hearts. So, lest we forget, let the steps be taken again and throw the footprints on the screen of eternity, and let the bells forever ring. But silent they will be unless the clappers resound against the metal to let the world know our bonds are more enduring than steel, and we the clappers be—Ring out, oh bells!

Bibliography

"A Survey of Southern Baptist Progress." *The Quarterly Review*. October, November, December, 1942.

"And The Crowd Goes Wild." *Celebrated Sporting Events*. Naperville, Illinois: Sourcebooks, Inc., 1999.

"The Ascent of Lost Man in Southern Baptist Preaching." *http://www.founders.org/FJ25/article1_fr.html*

Baker, Robert A. *The Story of the Sunday School Board*. Nashville: Convention Press, 1966.

"Baptist Hour History." *http://www.baptisthour.org/history.htm*

Baptist Message. April 29, 1938.

Baggett, James Alex. *So Great a Cloud of Witnesses: Union University 1823–2000*. Jackson, Tenn.: Union University Press, 2000.

Baring-Gould, Sabine. "Onward, Christian Soldiers." 1864

Brougher, Dr. J. Whitcomb, Jr. *Glendale Baptist Church*. Glendale, California, 1987.

Chicago Daily News. May 7, 1947.

Christian, John T. *History of Baptists of Louisiana*. Nashville: Baptist Sunday School Board, 1923.

Christian Index. February 24, 1944.

College Students. Adams Hall, Union University, Jackson, Tennessee, May 2, 1955, interview by author.

Commission. May, 1985.

"Dedicatory Message." Laying of the Cornerstone for New Educational Facility. C. Oscar Johnson, President of the Baptist World Alliance. First Baptist Church, Shreveport, Louisiana, May, 1949.

Dew, Emma. Poplar Grove Baptist Church, Brazil, Tennessee, May 1, 1955, interview by author.

Davis, Richard E. Trenton, Tennessee, May 1, 1955, interview by author.

"Dodd Faculty." *http://nobts.edu/campustour/cam003.htm*

Dodd, Monroe Elmon. *Baptist Principles and Practices*. Alexandria, La.: The Chronicle Publishing Company, 1916.

— — —.*Concerning the Collection: A Manual for Christian Stewardship*. New York: Fleming H. Revell Company, 1929.

— — —.*Girdling the Globe for God*. Shreveport, La.: John S. Ramond, 1935.

— — —.*Jesus Is Coming To Earth Again*. Chicago: Bible Institute Colportage Association, 1917.

— — —.*Radio Revival Sermons*. Kansas City, Mo.: The Western Baptist Publishing Company, 1932.

— — —.*The Democracy of the Saints*. Nashville: Sunday School Board of the Southern Baptist Convention, 1924.

— — —.*The Prayer Life of Jesus*. Nashville: Sunday School Board of the Southern Baptist Convention, 1923.

Dorm Director. Adams Hall, Union University, Jackson, Tennessee, May 2, 1955, interview by author.

Elder, Mrs. Harry. Trenton, Tennessee, May 1, 1955, interview with author.

Emedee. Yearbook, Dodd College. 1935.

Evening Leader. April 10, 1937.

Gandhi. Letter to Dr. and Mrs. Dodd. July 16, 1934.

Georgian. May 1, 1937.

Grafton, John. *America — A History of The First 500 Years*. New York: Crescent Books, 1992.

Greenville News. Greenville, South Carolina. October 5, 1935.

Grey, Dr. J. D. First Baptist Church, New Orleans, Louisiana, 1955, 1960, interview with author.

Hargrove, Mrs. Bond Shakeford. Trenton, Tennessee, May 1, 1955, interview with author.

Houston Chronicle. March 18, 1935.

Jones, Warren F. Union University, Jackson, Tennessee, May 2, 1955, interview with author.

Kingsport Times. October 24, 1937.

Los Angeles Times. August 31, 1940.

Loveless, Wendell P. "All Because of Calvary," © Copyright 1939 Hope Publishing Company, Carol Stream, IL. International Copyright Secured. All rights reserved.

McKinney, B. B. "Whisper a Prayer in the Morning."

National Voice. February 18, 1943.

New York Times. 1952.

New York Times. October 10, 1940.

Orr, J. Edwin. "Search Me, O God." 1869.

Ray, K. V. Franklin. President's Home at Union University. Jackson, Tennessee. May 2, 1955, interview with author.

"Reminiscence of a Baptist Minister." *http://funnelweb.utcc.utk.edu/-ddonahue/hestuff/azbill.htm*

Rodeheaver, Homer A. "He Lives" © Copyright 1933 Homer A. Rodeheaver, © renewed 1961 The Rodeheaver Co. (a Div. of Word, Inc.)/ASCAP. All rights reserved. Used by permission.

San Angelo Morning Standard. October 29, 1941.

Saturday Evening Post. April, 1983.

"75 Years 1923-1998 — An Anniversary Celebration." *Time* n.p.: Time Books, 1998.

"Shreveport/Bossier Historic Sites." *http://www.shreveport.net/sites/historic/*

Shreveport Journal. January 30, 1948.

Shreveport Journal. February, 1938.

Shreveport Times. February 10, 1935.

Shreveport Times. February 28, 1945.

Sibley, Mrs. R. M., Lurline Alison, and Fannie Pearl Colquitt. *History of First Baptist Church, Shreveport, Louisiana — "A Light Across the Century."* 1945.

Smith, Alfred B. "For God so Loved the World," © Copyright 1938 by Singspiration/ASCAP. All rights reserved. Used by permission of Benson Music Group, Inc.

Supervisor of Nursing. St. Mary's Hospital. Glendale, California, Summer 1987, interview with author.

Sykes, Seth. "Thank You, Lord," © Copyright 1940, renewal 1968 by Singspiration Music. All rights reserved. Used by permission.

Ticket Salesman. Railroad Station. Dyersburg, Tennessee, May 1, 1955, interview with author.

Toronto Daily Star. August 8, 1942.

Tremont Temple. Boston, Massachusetts, July 26, 1942.

"Union Impacts Baptist Heritage." *http://www.uu.edu/unionite/winter99/chlife.htm*

Waitress. Hotel Dining Room. Dyersburg, Tennessee, May 1, 1955, interview with author.

Young, G. A. "God Leads Us Along."

About the Author

JEWEL MAE DANIEL WAS BORN IN Vancouver, Washington, and reared in the Philippine Islands, San Francisco, California, and Texas. She was educated at San Marcos Baptist Academy in San Marcos, Texas; Baylor University in Waco, Texas; Southwest Texas University in San Marcos, Texas; and Southwestern Baptist Theological Seminary in Ft. Worth, Texas.

As an adolescent- and youth-education seminar speaker, Mrs. Daniel represented Southwestern Baptist Theological Seminary. She served as the youth and drama director for Dr. M. E. Dodd at First Baptist Church, Shreveport, Louisiana, writing plays and pageants for the theater department. She also served as Vacation Bible School director for both the Caddo Association in Shreveport and the state of Louisiana.

Mrs. Daniel also served on the Women's Missionary Union (WMU) Executive Board and as the state Christian education chairperson, at which time she wrote the state mission programs for the churches in Louisiana. She has been an inspirational and promotional speaker at WMU conventions, associational meetings, and men's and women's philanthropic organizations. She was also the women's chairperson for Louisiana College Crusade Region Three under President G. Earl Guinn.

Mrs. Daniel currently resides in San Antonio, Texas. She has three children and nine grandchildren.